Discard

OUR FATHER'S LIBRARY
38 W 2ND
PERU, IN. 46970

W9-BSE-564

THE LEADERSHIP LIBRARY
V O L U M E 7
HELPING THOSE WHO DON'T WANT HELP

THE LEADERSHIP LIBRARY

Volume
7

Helping Those Who Don't Want Help

Marshall Shelley

Carol Stream, Illinois

WORD BOOKS
PUBLISHER
WACO, TEXAS
A DIVISION OF
WORD, INCORPORATED

HELPING THOSE WHO DON'T WANT HELP

Copyright ©1986 by Christianity Today, Inc.

A LEADERSHIP/Word Book. Copublished by Christianity Today, Inc. and Word, Inc. Distributed by Word Books.

Cover art by Joe Van Severen

All rights reserved. Except for brief quotations in review, no part of this book may be reproduced in any form or transmitted in any form or by any means, electronic or mechanical, including photocopy, recording, or any information storage and retrieval system without written permission from the publisher.

Though the case histories that appear in this book are used with permission, names and certain identifying details have been changed in some to preserve the privacy of the parties involved.

Library of Congress Cataloging in Publication Data

Shelley, Marshall, 1953-
Helping Those Who Don't Want Help

(The Leadership Library; v. 7)
Includes bibliographical references.
1. Pastoral counseling. I. Title. II. Series.
BV4012.2.S49   1986   253.5   86-6855
ISBN 0-917463-10-2

Printed in the United States of America

To those who have shown me
  that love means
  knowing when to help
  even when help isn't requested.
To my parents and my pastors,
  who have guided not goaded,
  who have modeled godly initiative.

CONTENTS

INTRODUCTION

A man convinced against his will is of the same opinion still.

CHRISTOPHER MORLEY

A pastor encountered one of life's little dramas playing itself out as he entered the YMCA: A toddler wearing a wet bathing suit was coming out the door from the swimming pool area, and her mother was saying, "You are such a coward!"

The child was shivering, and her cheeks were wet — from tears or the pool? The pastor couldn't tell. She simply stood there shaking as her mother continued, "It's the same every week. You always make your daddy and me ashamed. Sometimes I can't believe you're my daughter." The pastor found himself thinking, *I wonder what the penalty is for hitting a woman?*

"What she was doing was more hurtful, more brutal than a beating," the pastor reflected. "It was emotional child abuse, and if it continues, that toddler will grow up feeling worthless, which will lead to all kinds of destructive behavior."

If that woman had been a member of your congregation, what would you have done? Most pastors feel the urge to do *something*, either immediately or eventually, to help the mother realize what's at stake, to help her be a better parent. Even if she isn't asking for help.

Can you help those who aren't asking for help? The question faces ministers in countless other situations.

A Church of Christ minister in Texas wrote LEADERSHIP recently, "For me, the toughest counseling problems are those where the changing needs to be done by someone other than the one I am counseling. For instance, the wife has come for help, but the husband is the alcoholic. Or the mother-in-law is a hypochondriac, but the daughter-in-law has come to you. How do you help in those situations? Should the problem person be confronted?"

Another pastor wrote, "My toughest cases are couples who come for 'help' after they've already decided to separate or divorce. They want to be able to say they tried counseling, but in actuality, they want approval for their divorce rather than any reconciliation or healing."

Yet another wrote, "How do you diagnose hurting marriages when they are 'hell-bent on hiding it'? How do you offer redemptive options when folks are too self-conscious to admit their marriage is failing?"

Counseling books usually offer tools for assisting those who want help, but what do you do for people who need help but aren't asking for any? Perhaps they don't know they have a problem. Or perhaps they know but refuse to admit it.

Almost every pastor knows the man, for instance, who takes his wife for granted and puts his marriage on autopilot, unaware or unconcerned that his wife is starving emotionally. Or the single woman who bounces from one job (or relationship) to the next, never satisfied, always looking for something else. Or the parents whose approach to raising their children is harmful (either tyrannical or uncaring). Or the engaged couples in premarital counseling who are blind to some serious areas of incompatibility.

These people aren't candidates for church discipline. Theirs is either self-destructive behavior (which they don't even recognize themselves) or else their problem is a sin of omission rather than commission, which makes overt discipline almost impossible.

This book focuses on the questions: When is intervention appropriate? What is the line between personal privacy and pastoral responsibility? How do I enter a situation when I'm uninvited?

This book will not answer all the questions; the situations are too complex. But it will show how other ministers are dealing with these situations. The stories and insights in this book are real. They have been gleaned from scores of interviews with pastors and Christian counselors. Names and identifying details have been changed in a number of the accounts to protect the privacy of those involved, but even with camouflage, these stories show the state of the art in "the ministry of taking the first step."

Volume 1 of THE LEADERSHIP LIBRARY dealt with *Well-Intentioned Dragons* — those individuals who sincerely believe they are serving God but who wind up being antagonists who wreak destruction. This book is not about those who attack the pastor but those who shy away from pastoral care. To borrow a football metaphor, pastors find themselves, at different times, having to play both defense and offense. *Dragons* was the game plan for the defensive squad. This book chalks a strategy for the offense.

It is not the final word on this subject; it is more like the first word. Hopefully, this book will spark additional thinking, writing, and refining of the skills necessary when ministers must take the initiative.

A number of situations demanding intervention remain untouched by this book — alcoholism, for instance, or chemical addictions, eating disorders, wife abuse, child abuse. Though these are certainly situations where help is needed and rarely sought, other books have dealt with these significant problems in greater depth than this volume ever could. (Some are listed in the Bibliography.)

This book covers those less dramatic but more common situations that pastors face virtually on a weekly basis. It uncovers some of the risks and the rewards of helping people who wouldn't think of asking for help.

ONE

THE HELPLESS HELPER

*I shall tell you a great secret, my friend.
Do not wait for the last judgment. It
takes place every day.*

ALBERT CAMUS

Working with people who don't want help can be confusing. It often leaves the would-be helper feeling helpless. The situations quickly become complex, and the appropriate response is rarely clear-cut.

To illustrate some of the complicating factors, this chapter is devoted to a single story of a pastor caught in this miasma. As you read the case study, try to imagine yourself in the shoes of this pastor, and try to answer these questions:

— What is the root issue?
— Do I have a responsibility here, or is this simply not my problem?
— Can the people involved be helped? Or do we just write them off?
— Would it help to call in someone else for assistance? Who?
— What, if anything, can be done?
— How long do you keep trying?
— Why do these situations cause my stomach to knot?

These were the questions going through the mind of one pastor not long ago. See how your responses compare with his.

At first, Brad Edwards had no reason to doubt Gil Farney. Gil and his wife, Penny, had come to the Bartlesburg Bible Church shortly after Brad had arrived as pastor three years ago. The Farneys sang in the choir and quickly were accepted into the congregational mainstream.

Thanks to his ready humor, Gil, a sales representative for a computer firm, made friends quickly. He had lost his left arm in an accident as a child, but he used his artificial arm as a conversation piece. He'd introduce himself by saying, "My name's Gil, but you can call me Stump."

Occasionally he would come to church with his artificial elbow bent backwards — just to see the reactions of people who didn't know about his arm. Those who knew Gil laughed with him.

The only flaw Brad had noticed was that Gil was something of a name dropper. Gil's cousin played professional baseball, and Gil managed to work that fact into more conversations than necessary, Brad thought. But he had to admit, he liked the tickets Gil finagled for the entire youth group the time his cousin's team came to town.

When Gil's company made some cutbacks and Gil lost his job, the whole church began praying for him. When the unemployment stretched into six months, then seven months, Brad could see Gil becoming more and more uncomfortable when people asked how the job search was going.

"Nothing yet," he'd say, "but my cousin knows some people with an independent TV station in Charlotte. There's a possibility of doing some weekend sports reporting."

A month later, Gil told Brad the job fell through because he'd had surgery to remove a cancerous growth in his stomach, and the TV station "didn't want to take a risk with someone like that."

It sounded strange, but Brad had no reason to doubt the story. Cancer wasn't usually a joking matter.

Brad asked how the Farneys were doing financially, and when he found out their car needed some repairs they couldn't afford, Brad dipped into his Discretionary Fund to pay the mechanic. Gil and Penny seemed grateful. "We'll pay the church back once we get on our feet," he said.

"Don't worry about it," said Brad. "We're glad we can help."

After another month with still no job, Gil would come to some informal social activities with alcohol on his breath. Brad wondered if he ought to say something, but he knew unemployment could be depressing. *It's probably better just to be the supporting family he needs right now,* he thought. *And help find him a job!* Brad began making some phone calls.

Before anything concrete developed, however, Gil stopped into Brad's office.

"I need to talk to somebody, Pastor," he began. "And I think I can trust you to keep this confidential."

"Sure. What's on your mind?" Brad asked.

Gil launched into an unusual story. "A guy I used to sell computers to found out I was unemployed. And through a middle man, he contacted me and asked me to think about setting fire to an old warehouse. I told him he was crazy, but he said, 'Just think about it. I'll make it worth your while.' I know arson's a crime, so I went to the State's attorney. The State's attorney took me over to the FBI, and they encouraged me to go ahead and meet the guy to find out what was going on." Gil paused. There was none of the jokester now. He was dead serious.

"So I met the guy, and we made arrangements to burn the place down. I secretly kept in touch with the FBI, and they were keeping me under surveillance. The night I was to torch the place, my friend told me to forget it — he was just testing me to see if I were willing. Then he told me he really wanted me to deliver some drugs." Gil was looking the pastor right in the eye, but his voice began to quaver. He looked frightened.

"Again, I contacted the FBI, and they told me to do what the guy said and to keep them informed. They wanted to see how many people were involved. That's where it stands now.

"I want to do what's right. I've agreed to help the FBI, but I need your prayers, Pastor. I'm scared, and I needed to talk to someone. I told the FBI about you, and they checked you out and gave me clearance to talk with you. So far, you and Penny are the only ones who know, and it's got to stay that way."

Not knowing what else to do, Brad agreed to pray for Gil and Penny.

Over the next few weeks, Gil stopped in periodically to give Brad updates. He told of staying out all hours of the night, making contacts for the FBI. His wife was being followed whenever she drove. His third-grade son was being tailed by the FBI to make sure he was safe. Their house was under surveillance from the vacant home across the street. Gil wove quite a web of intrigue. But, yes, he still needed a job.

When Brad talked with Penny, she confirmed the story. "Yes, I usually see a red car following me. It's scary, but Gil tells me those are the good guys. We've also had to have the phone taken out of the house because Gil was afraid it might be tapped."

"Is the FBI paying you anything?"

"Oh, no," she said. "I understand that would be illegal."

Brad continued to pray for the Farneys. It was all he could do. He didn't feel he could tell even his wife about Gil's situation. What if it were true?

Brad's phone calls did eventually find employment for Gil — a telephone sales job with a company that sold coupon booklets. It was a comedown for Gil, but at this point, he was happy for even a temporary situation. At least it was income.

Gil soon began telling Brad that other people at church were also involved with the FBI — some of them came to the services armed, he said. Brad began to be skeptical, but he couldn't confirm his suspicions. He couldn't prove Gil was a liar because everything was undercover. Brad doubted the FBI operated that way, but he was sure if he called they wouldn't tell him anything one way or the other. Brad found himself looking twice at every visitor who attended Sunday services.

Gil and Penny moved out of their rented house and into an apartment with Penny's sister and brother-in-law. It wasn't the best situation — two families with three kids in a three-bedroom apartment. But Gil told Brad, "We didn't have a choice. The owner of the house decided to sell, and the other apartments we've been looking at haven't been cleared by the FBI yet."

"Well, let us know when you find a place," said Brad. "We'll be glad to help you move the furniture."

The cramped living situation continued for three months. Seven people in one apartment made for some tension. Once when Brad was talking privately with Penny, she almost broke down. "I don't deserve to be treated like this. We're trying to help the FBI, and they're being unreasonable. Gil says every place he suggests, they veto. I don't know why God let us get tangled up in this."

Gil was also increasingly disturbed. Once he stopped in Brad's office visibly shaken. "Pastor, I'm afraid for my life. I had to go downtown late last night to contact some of the drug dealers. The FBI put a bug in my car so they could tail me, but when I got there, I realized the bug was gone. Someone had taken it! I couldn't see anyone tailing me, so I just drove away and came home."

Gil was pale. "They may kill me!"

Brad wished he had more facts, but Gil would never tell him whom to talk to with the FBI.

"Gil, you've got to get out of this situation. Get a lawyer."

"I tried, but they won't let me, Pastor. I just need you to keep praying."

Despite the inner turmoil, Penny and Gil appeared serene in public services at the church. No one but the pastor knew their story. He was glad when they did manage to find another house to rent. At least that was one problem solved.

About that time, Brad got a phone call from Molly Otter, the woman who had hired Gil, at Brad's request, for the telephone sales job. Molly attended another church but knew Brad from PTA.

"I'm afraid for Gil Farney," she began.

"Oh, why's that?" Brad asked.

"Something is bothering him. He's been drinking a lot on the job. One afternoon he was gone three hours and came back violently drunk, yelling at the others in the office, swearing at me, saying he was a loser and that I had hired a loser. He was out of control, and I was afraid he might hurt himself or someone else. I had another worker drive him home. I suspect the problem is his family situation."

"What situation? The apartment?" Brad asked.

"No, the divorce. I assumed you knew. He said he talked to you regularly."

"Tell me what he's told you," Brad said.

"For the last month or so, about every other day he becomes very distraught. Almost teary-eyed, he says virtually the same thing each time: Penny is divorcing him and going to take the kids, and he can't stand to see the family break up. Yesterday one of the other employees wanted to take up a collection to help him get an attorney. That's why I'm calling — to see if you can help us understand the situation."

"This is news to me," said Brad. "I know he's under pressure." He thought of one conversation with Penny when she had said, "I'm thinking of moving out of state until this thing with the FBI is over. I can't take much more." But that didn't sound like divorce.

"I didn't know Penny was leaving," he told Molly.

"Oh, yes. Two weeks ago they went out for lunch on his birthday. When Gil came back, he just sat there, staring at his desk. I asked what was wrong, and he told us all that Penny had just told him she was starting divorce proceedings. We were ready to lynch her — after all, breaking it to him on his birthday! I tell you, whenever she's come to the office since, everyone has given her the cold shoulder."

"Molly, I appreciate your call. Let me check this out."

"Brad," Molly said urgently. "You can't let him know I've talked to you. This has got to be confidential. If he knew I told you, it would destroy our working relationship. He's a good salesman, and they're hard to find. Promise me."

"All right, and again, thanks for calling." Brad hung up and immediately drove over to the house.

Penny opened the door. Brad smiled and said he'd just stopped by for a "pastoral call." She was alone and invited him in, and after a few minutes of small talk, he said, "Penny, you all lived with your sister for three months, and it was pretty cramped for you. That's a tough condition for any marriage. How are things going between you and Gil?"

"Much better now that we've got our own place," she said. "I think things are going to work out."

"I'm glad to hear that," said Brad, but inwardly he groaned. Gil's story about the divorce was a lie. He wondered how much more was fabricated as well.

Gil walked in a moment later, stumbling slightly as he walked through the door. Brad could smell alcohol. He realized he had a problem, a severe problem, on his hands. But how could he confront Gil about the divorce story without breaking his promise to Molly? He didn't feel, at that point, he could break the confidence.

"You've been drinking," he said to Gil.

"Yes," Gil admitted, sitting down dejectedly. "I don't want to, but after too much time with those FBI guys, I just have to drink to unwind."

By now, Brad was doubting the whole story. "Gil, you've got to quit. This thing is destroying you. Your spiritual life is threatened; your emotional life is a wreck. You've got to tell them you're through."

Penny was crying. And Gil looked at her and said, "You're right, you're right." Unable to use evidence of Gil's lies, Brad didn't know what else to do, so he offered a prayer and said good-bye.

Over the next few days, Brad did some investigation. Through a lawyer friend at the county seat, he discovered the Farneys' former landlord had not "sold the house out from under them." He had evicted them for nonpayment of rent.

In conversations with Molly, he discovered that Gil had refused the group insurance her company offered. "He told us he was still covered by his former employer," she said. "He wanted us to give him the money the company would have contributed to the group plan. We declined." Brad later determined Gil was not covered by any insurance plan.

Molly was flabbergasted when Brad told her Gil's story about Penny divorcing him was a lie.

"I can't believe it!" she said. "He would literally be crying after having lunch with her. Everyone in our office hated Penny for putting him through that. The few times she came in, we never said a word to her."

Molly was the first to confront Gil, and right away he said, "You've been talking to Brad Edwards." He didn't admit he had told a lie; he simply refused to talk about it. Molly didn't fire him, but she said she didn't want to hear any more about the divorce, and if he ever didn't show up for work, or showed up drunk, he was fired.

Brad also talked to him. Gil never confessed any falsehood; he tried to downplay it. Afterward Molly and Brad discussed the situation. "I think things are going to be OK," Molly said. "He's settled down at work. Let's not rock the boat."

Brad wondered what he should tell Penny — if anything. She didn't know about the divorce story. She still believed the FBI story. What should he do? He knew Gil had lied about the divorce, but he had no evidence to refute the FBI tale. Penny was somewhat emotionally unstable anyway, given to periods of tears. *If she found out what her husband had been doing to her, she might have a breakdown,* Brad reasoned. In the end, he decided it was better not to risk the trauma, at least not now.

And things did seem to get better — for a while. Gil continued to come to church every Sunday. He stopped telling Brad any stories about the FBI. He started helping with a Thursday night church program for boys, and faithfully attended, although Brad did notice he reeked of after-shave lotion. He wondered if it was to mask the smell of alcohol.

But after two months, suddenly Brad got a phone call from Penny's sister. "Would you please go see Penny? I think she needs you right now," she said mysteriously. Since the Farneys still had no phone, Brad drove over to their house.

Penny told him Gil had split. "Yesterday morning he woke up and told me he was going out to New Mexico, where he has some relatives, to look for a job," she said. "In two hours, he was gone. I haven't heard from him since, and I'm getting scared."

Brad tried to assure her things would be OK. He went back to the church and called Molly.

"Is Gil at work today?"

"No, and he wasn't here yesterday either. He called in to say Penny was pushing him for divorce again, and he had to see his lawyer yesterday and be in court today. He said to expect him tomorrow."

"Don't," said Brad. "It's a lie. He may be in New Mexico, but I don't even know that for sure."

At that point Brad went back to see Penny and told her everything — about the divorce story, his suspicions about the FBI yarn, everything. "Gil needs professional help," he said. "He's having trouble with alcohol. He's not facing reality. He doesn't even know what the truth is anymore."

Penny almost collapsed. She was sitting on the couch, but all the muscles in her body seemed to go limp. Then she began to cry hysterically, "I hate you. I hate you. I hate you." Brad let her shout until she calmed down.

He arranged for another woman in the church to stay with Penny and the kids. He also ordered a phone for their home so Penny could contact him or her sister. The only hitch was clearing up a past-due bill from a year before. Penny was shocked it was so easy; she still assumed the FBI didn't want them to have a phone. She worried that drug dealers might make threatening calls. Brad tried to assure her that no drug dealers or agents would be calling.

The day after the phone was in, Penny called in tears. "Pastor, you've got to come over!"

"What's wrong?"

"I just tried looking up your number in the book. I haven't used a phone in so long, I can't handle it."

Brad saw the tension and emotional strain Penny had suffered was greater than he realized. He looked in on her every day after that as she rode an emotional roller coaster — one minute thanking him for supporting her and the next minute accusing him of driving her husband away. Brad carefully explained that *when* (not if) Gil returned, she *had* to help him get professional counseling. "He's a sick man. We'll help with the costs," Brad assured her.

When Molly heard the emotional abuse Penny had suffered and the financial straits she was in, she brought her a check for $1,000 — the company contribution to the group insurance that she had refused to give Gil.

Two days later, on Friday when Brad stopped by the house, Gil was there. He'd rolled in the previous night. Penny didn't even greet the pastor; she just gave him a hard look and said, "It's his word against yours. How do I know you're not lying? And even if you're telling the truth, how do you know the people you talked to aren't lying?"

Brad didn't bother to defend himself. He turned to Gil.

"You need help, Gil. You have some problems I'm not capable of dealing with, but I can get you in touch with those who can."

"I'll be OK," he said. "I just need to get to New Mexico. I've got a job lined up that'll be great. We'll be near my folks."

"Gil, you have problems that New Mexico won't solve," Brad said softly. "You have trouble facing reality. You told people Penny was divorcing you. That's not true. You're telling lies. You're drinking . . ."

"I know, I know," said Gil. "Ever since I lost my job, I've felt confused."

"We'll get you help," said Brad.

"But I don't know what to do," said Gil. "We're getting evicted next Monday." That was the first Brad had heard about that. Another lie? He closed the conversation encouraged that at least Gil was open to counseling.

When he checked out the eviction story, his lawyer friend confirmed it. The eviction notice had arrived the day before

Gil had taken off for New Mexico. Brad speculated the two events were not unrelated.

Two days later, on Sunday, the Farneys were in church, greeting friends in the foyer as if nothing were wrong. Brad made a point to say quietly to Gil, "Let's get together tomorrow. We'll work things out."

"Sure," said Gil.

But the next day, when Brad went to the house, it was vacant. Even the furniture was gone. A call to Penny's sister confirmed that Gil and Penny had moved out Sunday night, heading for New Mexico.

Brad Edwards has not seen them since, although he has a hard time getting them out of his mind.

"Gil was one of the most jovial, easy-going men I've known," he says, shaking his head. "I still don't know what all was involved. It's probably a combination of the unemployment, midlife, depression, economic problems, the drinking, possibly problems between him and Penny, a self-image thing with his arm — who knows? All I know is that he desperately needed help, and I couldn't get him to accept it."

Not all situations pastors face are this dramatic, but many are equally frustrating.

When people don't want help, it's hard to get the facts, as Brad Edwards discovered. Sometimes people lie intentionally. Other times people are sincere, but their observations are inaccurate. How do you know who's telling the truth?

When you do get the facts — the right ones, hopefully — what can you do? How strongly do you come on?

And whose needs do you consider first — the Pennys, innocent bystanders, or the Gils, who desperately need help but create situations where help is almost impossible to provide?

As this real-life episode shows, helping those who don't want help is a complicated ministry. But as the rest of this book will show, it is possible.

T W O
WHY TRY?

One of the tests of leadership is to recognize a problem before it becomes an emergency.

ARNOLD GLASOW

The pain of seeing people who need help refuse to accept it is an affliction most pastors have experienced. But this must-help/can't-help dilemma is a struggle few others in the congregation sense — at least to the degree pastors do.

One pastor was concerned about several families in his church that always seemed to have financial problems. The problem was not unemployment; the families' incomes were adequate. They simply could not manage the money they made. They were harassed by collection agencies. They were facing foreclosure on their homes and personal bankruptcy. What could the pastor do?

About that time, two accountants in the church stopped in to see the pastor and offer their services to anyone in the church who would benefit from financial counsel in budgeting, spending, investing — all free, no strings attached. Since the pastor knew both men well, he knew their offer was free of ulterior motives to sell insurance or mutual funds or their accounting services. They simply wanted to offer their skills "as unto the Lord."

It seemed a perfect solution. Soon the pastor had arranged a series of meetings with the financially strapped families and the two accountants. The men helped them identify their expenses, set budgets, and work out a timetable for paying bills. They even contacted some of the creditors to forestall the foreclosures and said, "We've been asked to help manage the Smith family's finances, and we understand they are delinquent in their account with you. We've worked out a schedule for them to pay off their debt. . . ." Most creditors were glad to cooperate.

Things appeared to be going well. "I'm encouraged," one accountant told the pastor. "These people make enough money. It's just a matter of showing them where it needs to go." Each week, the families were to report their expenditures to the accountants.

The first week progressed according to plan. So did the second week. But by the third week, things started falling apart. One family drove up in a new Oldsmobile.

"We had to buy it," they claimed. "Our old car needed new tires and a tune-up anyway, so we figured we might as well put the money on a nicer car." The accountant buried his face in his hands.

Over the next few weeks, each of the families managed somehow to demolish the neatly organized budgets they had constructed. With the creditors and collection agencies no longer hounding them, they felt free to spend again.

Finally the two accountants stopped by the church office. "We're going to have to withdraw our offer to help with financial counseling. It's too frustrating to spend all this time with people and have them not follow through. Their spending habits are too deeply ingrained. We're glad to have tried this, Pastor, just to see what you have to put up with all the time. But we can't go on."

The pastor understood their frustration. But their response was also an encouragement. He recognized one of the unique characteristics required of a pastor — perhaps a sign of the pastoral gift — is a willingness to love people even when they initially rebuff that love. The two accountants did not possess that willingness.

Why We're Reluctant to Help

Even pastors grow impatient with resistant people. When I told one minister I was writing a book called *Helping Those Who Don't Want Help*, he said, "That's going to be the world's shortest book. You can't help people who don't want help. Jesus said, 'They that be whole need not a physician. . . . I am not come to call the righteous but sinners to repentance' (Matt. 9:12–13). Only those who recognize their need can be helped to change their lives."

It was a brief conversation.

But he raised an important point. Isn't it a bit presumptuous to think we can soften a hard heart or bend an unyielding attitude?

Another pastor said, "I work with the well and the willing. Most pastors spend too much time with the sick and the cynical."

Yet another said, "The danger in helping these people is that I communicate the situation is *my* responsibility when it's not. I cannot ultimately be responsible for others' behavior. It's *their* responsibility."

There are other reasons we're often reluctant to step in and offer help.

One is the respect — almost worship — we have in Western culture for individual rights. It seems almost a sacrilege to violate a person's desire to live life any way he chooses.

One group that has been able to get past this cultural do-not-disturb-my-lifestyle sign has been Alcoholics Anonymous. They are often called in by family members who feel the alcoholic is destroying himself and the family. Their intervention technique involves the family members and others whose lives have been affected by the alcoholic's behavior confronting him as a group — "ganging up" to point out how his behavior has hurt them and him, and insisting he get treatment. Though, in a sense, it violates his desire to live the way he wants, the AA technique is remarkably successful.

Another reason we are reluctant to confront people about their need for help is inertia. Pastors seldom have to "drum up business." There's usually more than enough business, or at least busyness, demanding their attention every day. With so many people knocking on your door, it's hard to get motivated to knock on someone else's.

Yet another reason is fear of personal rejection. Said one veteran pastor, "Most of us pastors greatly fear personal rejection because we're trained to be people pleasers. And to some extent we have to be — we have to maintain an ongoing, long-term ministry relationship with people."

But beyond fear of personal rejection, often just plain ol' fear of physical violence enters in. You can get into dangerous situations when you step in to mediate disputes, reconcile the rebellious, or protect people from themselves. A Presbyterian pastor from Cincinnati tells one such incident:

One night a woman called to tell me her husband was seeing a young widow from our church. She told me he was there even as we spoke! Even though it was 11:30 P.M., I drove by that widow's house and saw his car parked five doors away. It was the middle of winter, and I wasn't sure if I was shivering from the cold or from having to go up and knock on that door. I kept stalling and praying — it was about midnight by the time I knocked. Sure enough, there he was. He saw me, and he knew you don't make pastoral calls at midnight. I tried to appear calm, but I want to tell you — I was so scared you could have jumped rope with my intestines. I just said, "I need to ask what's going on."

He exploded: "Why are you meddling here?"

I said, "I'm here because I care about the two of you. I care about what this is doing to you and your children and to a marriage and to our fellowship in the church." This led to thirty minutes of tense and difficult discussion.

I eventually had to confront him again a few nights later in that home. I didn't have to say a word, because I knocked on that door and they didn't answer for a long time. When they finally answered, all kinds of guilt and hurt were uncovered.

The young widow was salvaged eventually from a bad situation and later married a wonderful man. Sadly, the man involved not only divorced his wife and left the church, but has since divorced a second wife.

It is the risk — physical and legal — of precisely such situations that causes many pastors not to take the initiative to make such "house calls." Other pastors minimize these risks, and with them their reluctance to act, by carefully avoiding the Lone Ranger approach and making sure to involve other mature leaders in the church.

When Pastor George Bradley began hearing rumors of an affair between two members of his Portland, Maine, congregation — both married, both active in the church — his first step was to talk with two of his trusted elders. With their support and assistance, he tried to piece together the story. When he was convinced the rumors did have substance, he went *with the two elders*, to ask the people involved if the stories were true.

The man brusquely told the pastor, "This is none of your business."

The woman confessed the affair and indicated she wished it had never begun but said that she was now "emotionally involved." She wasn't sure she would be able to simply turn her back on the man.

At that point, the pastor asked the whole board for counsel and prayer. Individual elders took the initiative to meet both with the offenders and the offended spouses to listen and to encourage them to maintain their marriages. "We're with you, not against you," the elders tried to communicate. "We want to save your marriage and prevent your kids from having to cope with a broken home." When these private, low-key encounters failed to stop the affair, the board gradually became more and more directive, working primarily with the woman, who at least admitted the affair was wrong and ultimately destructive even though she couldn't bring herself to break it off.

When the elders and pastor suggested the only solution might be for the family to relocate, the woman's husband agreed, and the board went to the extent of finding employment and another church for them in another state. They moved, and the thousand-mile separation finally ended the affair.

Both marriages survived. The family that moved has kept in contact with the home church and has expressed gratitude for the efforts of the pastor and board. The man involved in the affair also stayed with his wife. The two of them eventually left the church to join another one in town, but they are now active there, and their marriage is intact.

This is an unusual story, but Pastor Bradley minimized the risks. The whole board moved in concert. It was a group effort, not a solo rescue. The process was deliberate and well-planned, and thus avoided most of the risks involved in hasty intervention.

In addition to physical and legal dangers inherent in confronting people, at least three other dynamics are at work.

1. *Discomfort with repeat offenders.* In many cases, people who don't want help have "besetting sins," and those have always posed a problem for Christians. The term comes from Hebrews 12:1, which in the King James version, refers to "the sin which doth so easily beset us." Whatever the writer may have intended, the term has come to refer to a continual, repeated sin.

One church leader describes it: "Mary continues to have temper tantrums, Bill continues to get drunk [and] . . . Suzanne is into her fifth affair, even though each seemed to have repented, claimed victory, been resanctified (if such a thing is possible) or whatever. And it is the repetitiveness that throws us. We begin to avoid such people . . . placing them in a class apart from the rest of us who can at least manage to keep up appearances."[1]

Does God forgive a sin if we turn around and commit the

same sin again . . . and again . . . and again? In the abstract, most Christians will say "Yes, because we're all imperfect specimens, and God forgives and heals even habitual sin." But when it comes to specific sins, from which the person does not cease and desist — such as a pornographic addiction or promiscuity or ongoing bitterness — we wonder if true repentance has taken place. Those who don't "live in victory" are suspected of being devoid of spiritual life at all.

As a result, many of those with "besetting sins" keep their condition a secret as long as they can, wanting help, perhaps, but not the inevitable condemnation. And frequently the rest of us passively aid the cover-up because we too prefer not to know. Who wants to be bothered by the embarrassment or the general mess?

But as John White writes, "They are our wounded brothers and sisters. They are the church's closest pariahs."[2]

2. *Fear that we may have to negotiate the non-negotiables.* When trying to appeal to resistant people, some pastors fear they'll wind up adjusting the gospel to please those individuals. At times there may be a temptation to give away too much in our attempt to reach the rebellious. We lower our expectations. We can be tempted to "meet their needs" with a watered-down gospel rather than help them experience the truly transformed life.

As Oswald Chambers writes in *The Psychology of Redemption,* "We begin all right, but we get switched off. If we do not continue to live in the right place, we will get back into 'Adam sympathies.' . . . Satan's temptations of our Lord were based on sympathy with the first Adam — 'Put men's needs first.' Jesus says — 'Do not think first of the needs of people; think first of the commands of God' " (Mark 12:29–31).

In our desire to get people to accept the gospel and live accordingly, we dare not create simply a gospel that is acceptable to people.

3. *An assumption that a person's actions and attitudes are willfully chosen.* Yes, there is an inherent conflict between a person's fleshly desires and the commands of God, between the

old nature and the new. Again, Chambers writes, "The temptation to woo and win men is the most subtle of all, and it is that 'line' that commends itself to us naturally. But you cannot woo and win a mutiny; it is absolutely impossible. You cannot woo and win the man who, when he recognizes the rule of God, detests it. The Gospel of Jesus Christ always marks the line of demarcation."

Many times this kind of with-us-or-against-us thinking makes us reluctant to offer help. We assume the person has chosen to be the way he or she is. As we will see later, this assumption at times is valid, but other times it is not.

Why We're Obligated to Help

Are we kidding ourselves? Is this book built on a false premise — that we can solve other people's problems? Is there a compelling reason to take the initiative with people who are not overtly asking for help?

Despite the arguments against doing so, most pastors feel an obligation to help those who don't want help. Why? Their reasons fell into five categories:

1. *Because we all needed help before we wanted it.* The message of the Bible is that "when we were yet without strength . . . Christ died for the ungodly" (Rom. 5:6, KJV) and "God demonstrates his own love for us in this: While we were still sinners, Christ died for us" (Rom. 5:8).

At times, people may not want help because they are unable to want it — at least for the time being.

Vernon Grounds says one Bible text especially important to him is Job 6:14 — "A despairing man should have the devotion of his friends, even though he forsakes the fear of the Almighty."

"One of the ministries I consider my most meaningful," he says, "has been keeping in touch with friends who, over the years, have deviated from the faith — leaving the ministry or getting embroiled in a moral issue. I try to hang on to them without being obnoxious. I maintain some contact — sending a birthday card, dropping them an occasional note — always nonjudgmental, simply letting them know someone cares and is willing to listen. They know where I stand, but I'm not going to force myself or certain clichés on them."

Sin's effects can be described in two ways: indirect damage and direct damage. Indirect damage is the effect the sin has on people affected by the sinner. Direct damage is the person's increasing insensitivity to God, a growing blindness to the effects of his own sin. Conscience can become seared and eventually die.

Why help people who don't want help? Because we may be able to prevent indirect damage to innocent people (like Penny Farney in chapter 1). And because we may be able to prevent further direct damage to the spiritual sensitivity of the person himself.

2. Because love takes the initiative. Time after time, pastors referred to the biblical metaphor of the shepherd.

"Good shepherds see the wolf before the flock does. Just because people may not be conscious of a problem is no reason to avoid dealing with it," said one minister.

"As a pastor, I'm a shepherd," said another. "A shepherd doesn't say, 'I'll protect you from this ground hog, but not from that bear.' We have a job to do — to lead, guide, and protect — whether we like to or not."

One of the demands of leadership is to recognize problems before they become emergencies, and likewise, one of the challenges of ministry is to help people even before they recognize they're heading for the rocks.

Ray Stedman recalls a quotation from Dallas Cowboys coach Tom Landry: "The job of a football coach is to make men do what they don't want to do, in order to achieve what they've always wanted to be." Stedman then says, "I think that's also God's business with us — to make us sometimes do what we don't want to do in order to be what we've always wanted to be."

Throughout the Bible, love is shown taking the initiative even with people in rebellion. God repeatedly takes the first step, and second, and third. . . . He is not aloof, uncaring. He suffers the indignation of appealing to an uncaring world. Pastors often pointed to this image.

"I take Jesus as a model," says Roland Reimer of First Mennonite Brethren Church in Wichita, Kansas. "He reaches out and tries to help individuals either become aware of their need or, when they've given up, realize there is a way out of their problem. For example, when Jesus talked at the well with the woman of Samaria, he took the initiative, fought through her barriers, and opened the doors for her to heal her relationships. He definitely took the initiative with someone who wasn't seeking him out."

"With youth leaders," adds Malcolm Cronk of Camelback Bible Church in Arizona, "we frequently say 'Look for the strays — the youngsters who withdraw from the group, who stand on the periphery.' And it's up to the leaders to see that they are noticed and enfolded. That's what it means to be a shepherd."

While the principle of the shepherd's initiative is implicit, the apostle Paul states directly: "If a man is overtaken in any trespass, you who are spiritual should restore him in a spirit of gentleness" (Gal. 6:1). He doesn't limit the responsibility only to those cases where the individuals want to be restored. The effort, the initiative, comes from "the spiritual."

3. Because of the nature of the church. Some issues, especially marriage, are personal but not private. Because of the nature of the church, pastors can point out that their professional obligation is to deal with any situation that affects the church body. And marital problems certainly do. Not only is the other spouse affected, but so are children, and eventually the whole church will suffer if this marriage is allowed to deteriorate.

Being a pastor is both an advantage and disadvantage in dealing with people who don't want help.

The disadvantages? In many cases, because of the size of the congregation, the pastor's contacts are wide but not too deep.

"It's very hard to confront or 'carefront' when you don't have a close relationship established," said an Arizona pastor. "In other words, I may observe a few things or I may have been told something, but when I only have lunch with a person once a year, it's pretty hard to be corrective. It often can appear that the only time you see people is to deal with some problem or discuss negative types of things."

On the other hand, the nature of the church offers a distinct advantage for pastors stepping into their people's lives. Most church members still have some respect for the office of pastor. It carries a measure of authority — provided it's used discreetly. It also gives a ready entrée into situations that would be extremely awkward for a mere friend to address.

"A wife told me her husband was having an affair. When I met with the husband, I was glad I was a pastor. The husband knew that as a professional, our conversation had certain confidences built in. He also knew I wasn't just a nosy intruder, but I had an obligation as a pastor to mind the spiritual and moral well-being of each member."

4. *Because people are not always rebels.* Motivations are not always consciously closed. People are as they are for a reason: perhaps they are imitating the behavior of a parent.

One woman, to manipulate her husband, would goad him into screaming at her, and then storm out of the house, drive away, and disappear for two or three days. When she came back, the husband would be so frantic and guilt-ridden that he would do whatever she wanted.

The pastor discovered the woman's mother had done the same thing. The woman was merely following the pattern she had grown up with. The pastor was able to step in, point out the destructive effects in the mother's life (a bitter divorce), and help the couple begin handling disputes in better ways.

Sometimes people *are* consciously closed, but perhaps it is only a temporary condition. Sometimes weariness brings hopelessness and resistance to help. When the weariness is dealt with, the person may open up. One pastor quoted Isaiah 50:4 — "The Sovereign Lord has given me an instructed tongue, to know the word that sustains the weary." Sustaining the weary can allow them to accept help.

Often other factors enter in: physical problems or metabolic disorders. Because we are both body and spirit, biochemical imbalances can affect the soul. Medical care, rest, and good nutrition may be the first steps to help restore a person's mental and emotional balance. Then, when a better sense of well-being and a higher energy level are achieved, the person may be willing to consider changes.

One pastor memorized Job 29:15–17 and frequently repeats it to himself — "I was eyes to the blind and feet to the lame. I was a father to the needy; I took up the case of the stranger. I broke the fangs of the wicked and snatched the victims from their teeth."

"At times my job seems to be stepping in with the coping skills necessary to deal with the present," he says. "When we've dealt with the pressing emergencies, then I can begin presenting alternate ways of looking at the situation. Change is more likely when people are able to see they have options."

People may not seem to want help initially, but when they finally realize there are people committed to them, they sometimes change their minds.

5. *Because pragmatically, people's lives have been turned around by someone stepping in.* Although the percentages may not be great, many individuals can be reached by loving initiative.

Dan Koch was pastoring in a small town in North Dakota when a member of the congregation took him aside after a Sunday morning service.

"Did you hear that Ed is suing Barth?"

"No, I haven't heard anything about it."

"Well, it's true. Maybe you should talk with Ed."

Both Ed and Barth were neighbors, long-time members of the church, and friends — or so Dan had always assumed. He couldn't imagine what would suddenly prompt a lawsuit. That week he stopped by Ed's farm, and as they toured the fields in Ed's pickup, Dan said, "I heard a rumor you're suing Barth. Is that true?"

"It sure is. And I'm going to get him good, too," Ed said with an anger uncharacteristic of the taciturn farmer.

"What happened?"

Ed explained that he was in his car, inspecting the fields, just as they were doing now. "I was looking at my winter wheat, and the next thing I knew, I looked up to see Barth's car coming at me. He apparently wasn't paying attention, and he wandered across the middle of the road. I swerved, but I couldn't avoid him, and we crashed. Fortunately, we weren't going too fast, and neither of us was hurt, but both of our cars were bent up pretty good."

"What's the problem?" asked Dan. "You're both insured, aren't you?"

"Barth has full coverage, but I have a $250 deductible. So his carelessness cost me $250 and a lot of aggravation. But he wouldn't pay me anything, so I'm suing."

Dan shook his head. "I don't understand, Ed. You don't need $250. The last time we talked money, your biggest concern was where to invest your IRAs. How can you do this? You're stirring up more than $250 worth of trouble."

"It's not just this," Ed said. "For twenty years in my dealings with Barth, I've been getting the short end of the stick." His knuckles were white as he gripped the steering wheel. "Let me tell you about the last time. A piece of property was going up for sale — the old Unruh place. They were going to sell that land at $400 an acre. You know I don't have cash lying around; most of my money is tied up in equipment, and I have to take out loans if I'm going to buy land. I only had one section. Barth has four sections, and he pays cash for his seed and equipment. He's got money in the bank.

"Well, when he found out I was ready to buy the Unruh place, he went to them and said, 'I'll pay you $450 an acre,' as if he needed more land. I really did need the land, and it was adjacent to my farm; it made sense to get it. I had to offer $500. Then he offered them $525. I countered with $550, and he boosted the price again to $575. I eventually wound up paying $600 an acre for that land — just because Barth kept raising the price. And that's the fourth time in twenty years he's done something like that to me."

Dan began to see there was more involved than finances.

As he left, he said, "If I were in your shoes, Ed, I'd probably feel just as angry. But the Bible still says Christians are not to drag one another into court. It won't help anything, and it will only make the whole town think our church is a bunch of hypocrites. I want you and Barth to meet with me and see if we can settle this like Christians."

Ed reluctantly agreed.

After talking with Barth, who also agreed to talk it over, Dan set up a meeting for the next night in the church office.

He had no idea how he was going to arrive at a fair settlement on the issue of the $250, and even less how he could heal the deeper rivalry between the two farmers. But he knew he had to try. If he didn't, the cause of Christ in that town would only sport another black eye.

When both men sat down in front of Dan's desk the next night, he said, "Now I understand there's a dispute here over $250. I also understand that the issue is much deeper than the $250 deductible on the insurance. Barth, you don't want to pay Ed $250 because you don't feel that it's your responsibility. Ed, you feel that Barth has been making life harder for you financially for many years, and now you see a way to get back at him. I understand the situation, and I can see you both have a case. But I also know that 1 Corinthians 6 is still in the Bible. It's a poor statement about our faith when Christians haul one another before magistrates."

Dan paused to take a breath. Both men were expressionless. He couldn't tell what they were thinking. Breathing a quick, silent prayer for a miracle, and not thinking of any other way to proceed, he said, "I'm going to leave this room, but I'm going to leave my Bible here. Two passages are marked — Matthew 5:21–26 and 1 Corinthians 6:1–11. I want you two men to stay here, read them, and not come out until you've worked this thing through. When you come out, I want you to agree you'll drop the resentment and the bitterness you feel toward one another."

With that Dan walked out, feeling like a teacher dealing with two schoolhouse kids. *What in the world are they going to do?* he wondered. He desperately prayed they wouldn't start a shoving match inside the office.

He waited outside for twenty minutes. Finally Ed and Barth walked out. Ed spoke first.

"Pastor, you're right. We have been pretty immature about this, and we want to work it out. We're brothers in the Lord, and this bitterness that has developed between us isn't right. We recognize that. We're going to start over."

Dan was simultaneously relieved and skeptical. One side of him said, *O ye of little faith,* and the other said, *I'll believe it when I see it.*

"All right," he said. "Let's do something to confirm this decision." So there on the front lawn of the church the three men held hands and prayed, asking for strength and perseverance to sustain this new promise to one another.

How did they do?

Now, six years later, Dan reports that things were not completely healed immediately, but the confrontation was a beginning.

"I hadn't noticed it before, but whenever Ed was a greeter at the front door on Sunday morning, Barth would walk around to enter at the back of the church to avoid having to shake Ed's hand. And Ed would avoid Barth whenever Barth was a greeter. After our confrontation, the next Sunday the two men stood side by side at the front door greeting worshipers. I realized I'd never seen that before. It was a real breakthrough. They were willing to work together."

It all came about as a result of Dan's risky decision to enter a situation where he had not been invited. In this case, the two men never really wanted to hate, but their fierce independence did not allow them to ask for help.

While there may be limits to how much we can help those who don't want help, the experience of many pastors shows it *is* possible to effect change. And the Bible itself seems to offer models of a love that takes the initiative even when it has not been invited.

We all know the tension: Dangers lurk if pride assumes we can do the Holy Spirit's work for him. We must admit early in the book: If a person consistently and absolutely refuses help, there's ultimately nothing we can do. But there are a number of significant steps that can be ventured before that point of final rejection. Those steps are what we turn to next.

---

1. John White and Ken Blue. *Healing the Wounded.* (Downers Grove, Ill.: InterVarsity, 1985) p. 166.
2. Ibid., p. 167.

TO INTERVENE OR NOT TO INTERVENE?

In one of George MacDonald's books, there is a woman who has met a sudden sorrow. "I wish I'd never been made!" she exclaims petulantly and bitterly: to which her friend quietly replies, "My dear, you're not made yet. You're only being made — and this is the Maker's process."

JAMES S. STEWART

Sometimes pastors regret stepping in. Despite pure motives and a deep desire to help, their well-intentioned intervention can at times do more harm than good.

Earl and Edna Waring were in their forties, and they were childless. David Lindquist, their pastor, also noticed — with everyone else — their penchant for public bickering.

In the adult Sunday school class, Earl would joke about looking forward to the church potluck "so I can finally get a decent meal." Edna would counter, "I'm just glad the church has a full-time janitor to clean the floor after you've eaten." The rest of the class would laugh nervously. The humor did not quite cover the barbed intent.

David wondered how he could help Earl and Edna relate to one another without continual put-downs. One day he stopped by their house and asked pointblank, "Sometimes you two seem unhappy with each other. Why is that?"

"We're not unhappy," Earl said.

"Around the church, people perceive you that way, and so do I," said David. "You bicker about money in Sunday school. You publicly ridicule each other's appearance. Last Sunday,

Earl, in front of your wife, you told me, 'Edna can't cook worth a lick, which wouldn't be so bad if she'd only make the beds, but she never does.' It's wearying. But even worse, I worry about what it's doing to your relationship."

Earl and Edna didn't seem to take it seriously. David left, but he was determined to try again. He knew that often people needed time to get used to the idea of dealing with a problem. Over the next few weeks, he visited Earl and Edna two more times, and each time he'd ask, "How are you two getting along?" Each time, they'd reply "Fine."

But David didn't give up. On the next visit, he pressed harder.

"There must be something underneath that's rankling you two. Earl, tell me, what attracted you to Edna in the first place?"

As Earl retold the story of their meeting, Edna remained strangely quiet, seemingly preoccupied. When he was done, David pressed her to open up, to describe her relationship with Earl.

After a long pause, she said, "Earl, I need to ask your forgiveness." She seemed to stumble for words. She began to talk about her past, revealing several rather sordid sexual experiences with various men before she had met Earl.

"I was quite a floozy," she said. "Maybe that's why I'm the way I am now. I've never been too domestic a lady. Of course, I'm saved now, and that puts everything away, but sometimes I still feel guilty."

Earl listened wide-eyed. "I never knew that before!"

"I appreciate you sharing that," said David, feeling that at last he'd made a breakthrough. "Earl, how about you? What experiences in the past may be continuing to influence the way you relate to your wife?"

Earl hung his head and admitted that he, too, had been rather promiscuous in his young adult years. He admitted he still was attracted to other women, although he had not actually been physically unfaithful.

David talked about forgiveness and accepting one another.

Before he left, he prayed with them that they would be able to support one another rather than tear each other down.

Unfortunately, the approach was a mistake — at least in that particular encounter. Now, ten years later, David wishes he had handled things differently.

"I got them to confess all this dirt to each other," he says. "But all it really did was create suspicion and distrust. 'Will she do it again?' 'Can he ever really put his past behind him?' They had been married about eight years at that point, and though they bickered, they had stayed together. But within another year, they were divorced."

Of course, they might have divorced anyway, but David feels his unwise, or perhaps untimely, intervention contributed to the failure of the marriage.

"Given their patterns of communication, I had simply added to the ammunition they could use against one another," he says. "They had learned to live with the bickering about cooking and unmade beds. That was a comfortable — and safe — way of fighting. But suddenly I'd introduced the heavy artillery, and even when it wasn't used overtly, it was always in mind, and that proved too weighty for the relationship to bear.

"For me," he reflects, "it raises the question of whether we really need to know everything in the past or not. Isn't the forgiveness of God sufficient not to raise those questions again?"

Seeking disclosure for disclosure's sake, he now feels, is a mistake.

David Lindquist's experience also raises another issue: At times, trying to help only hinders. If even well-intentioned intervention can prove destructive, when should a pastor intervene, and when should even a bad situation be left alone?

Obviously, even in small churches, there are going to be more fires flaring up, more problems in people's lives, than any pastor can personally stamp out. How do you decide which ones to take on?

When NOT to Intervene

There are occasions when it is probably best *not* to try to help those who don't want help.

When you don't know the person. Without some kind of personal relationship, intervention is difficult and risky. In these cases, the better strategy is an indirect approach.

"At the shopping center, I often see harried mothers ready to strike their toddlers or scream at them for simply being young and dropping their ice cream or whatever," said one woman, a co-minister with her husband. "Since I don't know them, I don't feel I have the right to directly intervene, but one time I walked by and said, 'They're a handful, aren't they? I'd forgotten how much patience it takes to be a parent. Even so, I wish my children were that age again. Yours are so cute.' It knocked the props out from under the mother. Suddenly she said, 'Yeah, they are kind of cute.' I was simply trying to be a little salt of the earth. We never exchanged names, and we may never meet again, but that compliment kept her from throttling her kids."

When you're beyond your depth. When a situation demands more skill or time than you have available, the best thing you can do for yourself *and* for the person is to bring in someone else.

One pastor found himself facing an impossibly complicated marriage triangle. Initially the wife came to the pastor complaining about poor communication patterns. When the pastor met with the husband, he discovered the man had been having an affair for over a year.

The problem was that the wife was pregnant, and so was the mistress! The husband didn't want to lose his family; he wanted to keep his wife. But he was not only emotionally attached to the mistress, he felt a moral responsibility to help her through the pregnancy and delivery of *their* child.

The pastor was stumped. "Normally, I'd tell a man to stop seeing his mistress as a prerequisite to rebuilding his marriage. But what could I do in this situation?"

When the husband started bringing the mistress to the pastor for counseling, the pastor knew it was time to call for reinforcements.

"I was in over my head," he said. "I think I know how to help couples repair their marriages, but I can't do that and help the husband and his lover at the same time."

Since the husband and wife were members of his church, he continued to see them, but he referred the mistress to another Christian counselor.

How can you tell when it's time to refer? Another pastor offers a helpful image: "I give it my best shot in two or three meetings to see if there are any indications of healing. I'm a counselor, not a psychotherapist. The difference: Counselc ⸳⸳ put bandages on the wounded so natural processes can helṭ them heal. But when a person is continually ripping the bandages off the wound so it will never heal, it's time for the psychotherapist."

Perhaps the best most pastors can do is clean out the dirt to prevent infection, apply bandages, and set up the situation where normal healing processes can work. When the person persistently sabotages that treatment, it's time to refer.

When your motivation isn't right. Motives are always mixed; elements of fear/love/worry/altruism/reputation all get tangled together when confronting a volatile situation. And yet, pastors have found that some of their most counterproductive confrontations take place when they've gone in with the wrong motivation. So they identify warning lights that occasionally tell them their motives are not right for intervention.

"I was once tempted to confront a husband about his misbehavior, but I realized the only reason was because I liked his wife. Instead of being an ambassador for Christ, I would have been the woman's advocate, her mouthpiece. I realized I was not the right one to counsel that family."

Other pastors admit the temptation to make an appointment with a woman to discuss a problem her husband had mentioned, motivated largely by the pleasure of being with her. In that case, too, the motive is probably sufficient to rule out personal involvement.

Another dangerous and ineffective motivation is self-righteousness. "I've found being dogmatic and legalistic does not lead a person to want help. It turns him against it," said a pastoral counselor. "But if he feels he'll get a fair hearing, he's much more apt to let someone step in. It's crucial to sincerely want to understand that person's point of view. Even if I wind up disagreeing with the decisions he makes, I want to know the factors that went into making those decisions."

Anger is yet another motivation that must be brought under control before attempting intervention. As Laurence J. Peter once said, "Speak when you're angry — and you'll make the best speech you'll ever regret."

Even when the individual has acted so badly as to deserve punishment, "you need to deal with your own feelings before you can deal effectively with the situation," says psychiatrist Louis McBurney. "It's natural to see a child abuser or workaholic as a real villain. But simply being judgmental will not help anyone. The only way I've found to get feelings under control so you can work with the person is to start asking *What's caused this person to act this way?* Everyone is part victim as well as part villain; every story has two sides. Obviously, we've got to get the individual to stop the destructive behavior, but to do that, we must understand what factors led him or her to act that way."

By checking emotions of anger and judgment, we can begin to truly listen and ask the right questions. McBurney observes, "At this point, you can form an alliance with that person, so he doesn't see you as being *against* him but *with* him, and often the person can say, 'I hate this about myself, too. I really do need help.' "

A final motivation pastors find they must guard against is seeing themselves as saviors.

"I have a standard speech for my staff I call 'Messiah Complex 101,' " says a pastor in the Southwest. "Everybody gets it several times because all of us in the helping professions have a little touch of the Messiah complex. We tend to believe that given enough time and money, we can love people enough and pray hard enough and work hard enough to help anybody. Not so. There are some people you cannot help no matter how hard you try. Everybody has to learn that, and if you don't, you can create more problems than you solve. Part of learning to be a minister is recognizing there are some people for whom you have nothing to offer — at least at this point in time."

How can you identify the people you *can* help? Do you have to try and see if you get rebuffed? Or can indications tip you off right from the beginning?

When TO Intervene

How do you discern the leading of the Spirit from a human compulsion to correct someone? Here are some of the factors pastors point to when deciding whether to help a person who doesn't want help.

God's persistent call. Opportunity does not equal a mandate to act. Just because you become aware of a need does not mean God is calling you to meet that need.

"I do not think God has called me to straighten out everyone," says one long-time pastor. "Unless it's an obvious emergency, I consider a concern God-given only if it stays with me over time. If it's a passing thing, I doubt if it's the call of God. But when the Lord lays it on your heart to help someone, he'll make sure you don't miss it. The story of young Samuel comes to mind. God will call you more than once if it really is of him."

Another pastor said, "In some cases, I've waited three weeks to six months before I knew God wanted me to act. He used that time to show me other facts I needed to know. I became more observant. I gained wisdom and necessary evidence."

When, before God, motives are right. If we are tempted to

"straighten someone out," it is doubly important to check our motivations. What *should* the motivation be? Because I love God. It sounds simple, and it is. But in essence, that has to be the primary motive: loving God and wanting to help others love God, too.

"One motivation I have to guard against is feeling pious and smug before God," said one pastor. "It's easy for me to point out misbehavior or sin because it makes me feel righteous. It's even sweeter when something bad happens to the person and I can say, 'Don't you remember when we talked about that? I warned you.' But that doesn't do the person any good, and it certainly doesn't help my spiritual life. It's pride, which leads to the Elijah syndrome — 'It's just you and me, Lord, and sometimes I wonder about you.' "

A check on that motivation is to ask, *Do I care deeply for that person, and not simply for the other people in the situation?* The guidance in Galatians 6, the passage that commands those who are spiritual to restore those who are "overtaken in a trespass," is all couched in language emphasizing the importance of eliminating any self-righteous tendencies. We are to "bear one another's burdens" (v. 2) and "watch yourself, or you also may be tempted" (v. 1) and not think too highly of ourselves (v. 3) and test our own actions (v. 4).

As counselor Everett Worthington, Jr., writes, "Only after careful self-examination — more than a cursory overview — praying in the presence of the Holy Spirit, can we see well enough to even attempt to remove the painful splinter from the eye of a friend. It is never hasty."[1]

Before attempting to correct anyone, he asks himself these questions to check his motivation:

- Do I really care for that person?
- Am I a close enough friend that I am willing to bear his or her burdens?
- Is the timing right for a confrontation?
- Is the Holy Spirit directing?

If the answer to all these is yes, then Worthington considers *how* to broach the topic. "The key is that we restore people 'in a spirit of gentleness,' lest we too be tempted (Gal. 6:1)," he writes. The danger to pride is ever present.

The timing is opportune because of a crisis. Often it's a matter of time before you break through to resistant people. And many times breakthrough arrives as a result of a crisis in their lives.

Ike, for instance, was a farmer and a father of the old school — strict with his children and never showing emotion. He would make his children line up when he entered the house, and he expected them to sit without speaking at the dinner table.

His pastor, Eb O'Malley, claimed he could never talk to Ike about anything personal. Ike was always polite but reserved; conversations were kept on a surface level . . . until Eb was called to perform the funeral of Ike's brother.

A few days later, Eb met Ike at lunchtime, and Ike said, "You know, my brother and I were very close. One reason was because we endured a lot together as kids. My father was a harsh man. When I was twelve, my mother died, and the day of her funeral my dad got us up early and forced us all to work in the field from 6:30 to 10:15. Then he called us in, and we had fifteen minutes to get dressed for the funeral. We went to the funeral home, and immediately after the service, he loaded us back in the car, brought us home, and sent us back out to the field. We couldn't even go to the dinner that everyone else was having after the funeral. I remember thinking *Aren't you supposed to cry when your mom dies?* But Dad never gave us a chance. He wanted to keep us busy."

Ike looked at his pastor. "After my brother's funeral a couple days ago, I got to thinking. Maybe I'm more like my father than I'd like to admit."

Eb said later, "From then on, he was much more willing to talk with me about his relationship with God, his wife, and his children. His brother's funeral seemed to be the turning point."

Sorting Out the Options

Most pastors, as they mature, begin to seek counsel before riding off on any rescue missions. As one pastor described it:

"Early in my ministry, I took a solve-them-as-they-come approach. My assumption was *we shouldn't have problems in this church,* so anything I became aware of I tried to solve. Even though my motive was good, my assumption was not well thought out. I never asked, 'How does this problem compare to this other problem, and which of the two should I be spending time on?' I didn't have any plan of action. As the bullets were fired, I tried to bite them. I about lost my sanity.

"In my second church, I began to trust the advice of my two part-time staff members. Before I acted, I'd sit down with them and discuss the situation. We would decide whether any action was necessary or not. If not, we'd pray about it and leave it. If we decided action was necessary, then we'd decide who and how, or if anyone else (such as the board) should be in on it."

Before taking the initiative in a ticklish ministry situation, this pastor and his associates asked themselves these questions:

1. Do we have all the facts? Do we have something more than hearsay? What can we do to get a fuller picture?

2. Once we have a better understanding of the situation, is it as bad as we thought? Whom does it really impact? Is it a church-wide problem? Is it going to affect one family, four families, or forty families?

3. Can we afford to wait? If we don't respond, what's the worst thing that could happen in a week? In a month? In a year?

"That's not passing the buck," said the pastor. "That's gaining the wisdom of time. You don't ignore it forever, but instead of rushing to the fire immediately, take some time to gain perspective. If we felt the problem could wait a month, we would let it go. My tendency was to exaggerate the urgency. I was surprised how many 'emergencies' took care of themselves in a month.

"If we had a limited problem involving three or four families, and we felt it was intense enough to require action, then we would assign one of the pastors to chat with the individual or the family and see what could be done.

"If we discovered forty families were being seriously affected, then we would bring it before the church board and say, 'Here are the facts as we understand them. Do any of you know anything we don't know or anything that would be helpful?' Then we would say, 'What do *you* think we should do?' "

Farmers know crops go through three stages: green, ripe, rotten. Harvest is effective only at one of the three stages. Pastors, too, have learned that intervention is not always the appropriate action, but at the right time, it can produce a rich spiritual harvest.

There's another lesson from the farm, however, that applies. For people to grow, they, like plants, demand an environment where growth is possible. You simply can't force growth out of corn by tugging on the stalks. To grow healthy plants you try to provide nutrients and protection from insects, but you don't keep pulling the plants up every day to check their progress.

So it is with people who don't want help. Sometimes the best thing we can do is provide an environment where change can take place. A steady, consistent witness is often more influential than stormy confrontations or attempts to create an artificial crisis.

So we turn to climate control.

---

1. Everett L. Worthington, Jr. *How to Help the Hurting.* (Downers Grove, Ill.: InterVarsity, 1985) pp. 48–51.

FOUR

AN ATMOSPHERE CONDUCIVE TO CHANGE

Men are free when they belong to a living, organic, believing community, active in fulfilling some unfulfilled, perhaps unrealized purpose. Not when they are escaping to some wild west.

D. H. LAWRENCE

There's an old story about a boy who found a turtle that had withdrawn into its shell. He tried to pry the turtle's head out with a stick. His uncle saw what was happening and said, "Not that way." He took the turtle inside and set him on the hearth. In a few minutes, as it began to get warm, the turtle stuck out its head and feet and calmly crawled toward the boy.

People, like turtles, can't be forced to open up. But in the right environment, they often choose to do so. Warmed by kindness and concern, they sometimes relax, and often wind up coming your way.

These are some of the ways pastors create an atmosphere conducive to personal change:

Dignify Pain and Suffering

Many people request help but resist it when it is offered. To be more precise, they want the pastor to take away their pain, but they don't want to deal with the underlying problems producing the pain. They don't want help if it means making changes in the way they're living.

"People seldom know the solution. But they know they are unhappy, and they can describe eloquently, with exquisite detail, how their lives are out of sync," observes Roger Thompson of Trinity Baptist Church in Wheat Ridge, Colorado.

In some cases, the problem hinges on a superficial view of pain, particularly emotional pain. They believe the absence of pain is an inalienable right. Even some pastors fall into this trap.

"Most people who deal with suffering, pastors prominent among them, are by training and temperament doers and fixers," says Eugene Peterson, a Presbyterian pastor in Maryland. "They want to do something about what is wrong with the world. Suffering is something wrong with a person — and they are prepared to do something about it."

Sometimes, however, the pain is not something to be avoided, cured, fixed. It may be entirely appropriate. In these situations, the absence of pain would be pathological.

One young man, Karl, came to his pastor frustrated because he wasn't "happy." He had just broken up with his girl friend, the company he worked for was struggling financially, his job was in jeopardy, and he was wondering what direction his life should take.

"He seemed to have the idea that life should always be blissful," said the pastor. "Karl's feelings of disquiet, which were quite normal, were intensified because he didn't think anyone should ever feel that way. But there would have been something wrong with him if he *weren't* feeling pain from a broken relationship and an uncertain job situation."

The pastor pointed Karl to the book of Lamentations, which faces suffering and uncertainty, takes the situation seriously, but doesn't *do* anything about it. No quick answers; no easy remedies. The pastor simply reminded Karl of God's faithfulness.

"I needed the message of Lamentations at that point, too," said the pastor. "It kept me from rushing in with 'therapy' for Karl. It kept me from the temptation to manipulate or alleviate, which is always condescending and belittles the person's pain. When the pain is legitimate and normal, I feel it's up to God to heal. My job is to give companionship, meaning, and dignity to the person in the midst of it."

Eugene Peterson suggests that pastors help people "lean into the pain" — to enlarge their capacity for suffering. "The pastor who substitutes cheery bromides for this companionship 'through the valley of deep shadows' can fairly be accused of cowardice. Writing cheerful graffiti on the rocks in the valley of deep shadows is no substitute for companionship with the person who must walk in the darkness."[1]

Help People Expect Trials

Despite most Christians agreeing, in principle, that life with Christ will not remain problem free, ample confusion remains over what kind of protection God's people will enjoy. Are they supposed to experience *peace*? How about *fulfillment* or *joy* or *assurance*? And what do these concepts mean when hormonal or emotional upheaval strikes?

"We often tend to neglect one of the key themes of Scripture," said one former pastor. "And that is: Walking with God does not mean you won't face problems, even emotional problems. If you'd tell a ten-year-old boy, 'Son, if you'll become a Christian, you'll never have to be a teenager,' we'd all see that as ridiculous. But I have heard people tell forty-year-olds, 'If you're really walking with God, you don't need to worry about menopause or midlife transition.' "

The "Any problem can be solved if you just get right with God" mentality simply doesn't square with most pastors' experience.

Being right with God, as far as confessing sins and walking in obedience, does not mean that you're going to have enough money to live on, or that your husband won't walk out on you. In fact, when you look at Scripture — Isaiah 43, Psalm 23, James 1 — you get the impression that the opposite is true: Those who walk with God will endure fiery trials.

One pastor experienced a real breakthrough with several

people in his congregation after preaching a series of messages on "Valley People."

"The point of the series was that the Bible teaches us to be faithful and sustain one another in the valleys as well as the mountain tops of Christian experience. I gave several examples of people who were faithful amid suffering and other examples of Christians who ministered to those who were suffering. In the two years since I preached that series, more people have referred back to that one than any other. It seems to have given people permission to be *real*, to recognize the 'elevation' of their emotions and life situation is constantly changing. They don't have to always wear a smile. God continues to be faithful whether we're on the peak or in the valley."

The pastors who communicate that trials are part of the Christian life, and that they are not a sign of God's displeasure, find the atmosphere is more conducive to people owning up to the pressures they face and being willing to accept help.

Encourage Healthy Self-Disclosure

One reason people often don't want help is because the vulnerability demanded in such an admission scares the tar out of them.

To overcome this, one nondenominational pastor shares "stories that show me in a negative light, and there are lots of them! People need to see my weaknesses, but more importantly, how I'm working on them. Men who are insensitive to their wives, for instance, need to see that I'm insensitive to my wife at times but, just as important, that *I'm trying not to be.* In one sermon I told about listening to my wife as she was telling a lengthy story. I finally said, 'Can you get to the bottom line?' It was rude. Tears trickled down her cheeks, and she said, 'I listen to you when you talk about sermon ideas and your plans for the upcoming week. I share my story, and all you do is ask me to get to the bottom line.'

"Or, not long ago I talked about family tensions. I told about going into my daughter's bedroom and telling her I was sorry about breaking a promise. She said, 'Dad, you say that more than anybody else in the family. But I guess you need to.' We both laughed. Then she said, 'I appreciate that about you, Dad.' "

Revealing weaknesses and failures isn't easy, but people identify with and benefit most from lessons learned through mistakes. Even Jesus offered his scars to doubtful Thomas, with powerful effect. Thomas believed and was reconciled after seeing for himself the effects of Christ's suffering. As Fulton Sheen once said, "Scarred men come for healing only to scarred hands. Only a Risen Jesus with scars can understand our hearts."

On the other hand, sharing personal victories in daily life can also be helpful.

Pastor David Korb one Sunday told the story of backing his car out of the garage and hearing a snap. He stopped and discovered his favorite fishing pole had been left behind the car. It now was in two pieces.

He walked into the house and asked, "Who was using my fishing pole?"

"I was, Dad," his five-year-old son said.

"Look at it now," Dave said, holding up the two pieces. "What happened?"

"I was playing with it and set it against the garage door. I forgot to put it away."

Dave realized it must have fallen down behind the car. He wasn't pleased, but neither was he going to cry over spilled milk — or broken poles.

"Well, thank you for telling me," he said quietly and went back to the car.

As Dave told his congregation: "I didn't think much more of it, but two days later, my wife told me that when she and our son were at Sears, he said, 'Mom, I've got to buy Dad a new fishing pole. I broke his other one. Here's my money.' And he handed her his savings of two dollars.

" 'That's nice of you to offer,' she said. 'But you don't have to do that.'

" 'I want to, Mom,' he said. 'I found out something. I found out that Dad loves me more than he loves his fishing pole.'

"When I heard that," Dave said, "I felt great. For once in my life, I had done something right."

After that sermon, several men told Dave, "I appreciate you saying 'For once I'd done something right.' That's refreshing coming from a pastor. I thought you always did things right at home."

Sharing that careful blend of humanness without false humility, victories sans pride, presents an authentic picture of God's work in a life. And that's one of the most important roles a sermon can play. Such illustrations demonstrate a pastor's willingness to own up to failures and work to improve them. They also set a tone that allows people to admit they need help, too.

Allow Others to Help You

Healthy relationships are two-way streets. One of the most affirming things we can do for people is to allow them to help us in some significant way — even to change us. When people see we have been affected by others, they're more likely to admit they need us as well.

One pastor found his preaching criticized with some regularity. A number of people told him he wasn't connecting. He set up a weekly Tuesday morning group of five men and women who would critique his sermon and — lest they become mere gripers — would help think through the passage for the next Sunday.

"I am open with the congregation about this group being there to help me preach better," says the pastor. "I had been criticized for fuzzy thinking. This group helps sharpen my ideas and gives me help with applications. Since I've submitted myself to them for help, I've noticed other people are more open to my taking the initiative to help them with problem areas in their lives."

Practice Preventive Counseling

"We counsel by the way we live," says veteran pastor Malcolm Cronk. "My lifestyle, my own marriage, my family, is part of my counseling. It says something. It isn't always articulated in formal statements, but it's there. People sense it."

One pastor described his whole ministry as "preventive counseling."

"I've had people tell me I'd saved their marriage. I didn't even know their marriage was in trouble. But what they meant was that by teaching the biblical view of marriage and by illustrating it with Christ's relationship to the church, they picked up principles to apply to their own marriage, and they worked it out."

Ministers plant seeds in soil plowed by life's circumstances. Many of the seeds take root. Some we're aware of; others we aren't. But by teaching biblical standards with biblical illustrations or illustrations from life, people beginning to go through those kinds of experiences often appropriate those principles. They experience the remedial effect of preventive counseling.

Preach to Affect the Climate

Effective preaching creates a healthy atmosphere where lives can be changed. It won't be done, usually, by one sermon. It's more the result of a steady, nutritious diet, the cumulative effect of consistent attitudes and applied theology expressed from the pulpit. Preaching can also be effective in dealing with specific situations.

Somebody once asked Gregory of Nazianzus a question. He replied, "I would rather answer that one in the pulpit!" At times there's a temptation to deal with people's needs from the safety and insulation of the pulpit rather than face them alone in the intimacy of a pastoral visit. Certainly personal contact is important, but the pulpit *can* be used to say things that simply cannot be said in one-to-one conversation.

"In a sermon I can talk about the urgency of committing ourselves today. It's time to put our lives on the line for

Christ," said a Baptist minister. "There are some people in this congregation who've never really given their lives to Christ, and they need to hear this occasionally. It would be difficult to say in a one-to-one conversation. One woman told me after a recent service 'I've known for some time that I needed to give my life fully to God, but it wasn't until today's sermon that I felt God telling me that this was the time.'"

Sometimes people who "don't want help" simply don't know how to ask for it. They may have some vague sense that things are not right, but they don't know there's a better way. They don't know what steps to take. How can you reach people like this? It's hard even to identify them at times.

The key, according to one minister, is often through describing the problems realistically from the pulpit. He recently preached a sermon on the temptation to lust. His approach was not "lust is disgusting — how could anyone who calls himself a Christian fall for a temptation like that?" Instead, he said, "I can understand why lust is such a difficult battle today. Our days are saturated with sex-oriented advertising and media. We've been conditioned to judge people by appearances, by the image they project. I'm tempted, too, especially when I'm feeling lonely or isolated." He went on to point out the self-consuming side of lust and how God offers freedom from this potential addiction.

The pastor reports: "After the service one man approached me and said, 'Your sermon made me realize I need to talk with you about this. I thought I was weird and crazy, that I was the only person in this church with this problem. You seem to understand the feelings. How do I learn to control them?'"

The pastor was able to offer some steps for help. Without the public presentation of the problem as a real but understandable temptation, the man would have continued to feel he had a unique, unsolvable penchant.

Perhaps the worst mistake a pastor can make is to belittle the struggles people face, or to suggest that "truly spiritual people" live above failure.

"Earlier in my ministry," said one pastor, "I kept talking

about 'victory' and how people could straighten out their lives if they would just resist temptation. Now, I still believe God can change lives, but in those days I'm afraid I was pretty cavalier about the process. I would say things like 'If there's a sin problem, deal with it. God can't protect you if you aren't walking with him.' The implication, of course, was that if you felt under attack, you weren't close enough to God.

"Recently, a woman who had been in the congregation back then told me about their child, who in those days was causing severe family stress. 'I wanted to come for counseling,' she said. 'But my husband said no, that we could work it out in the family. He thought you would only get mad at us for letting this problem develop.'

"I felt like I'd been stabbed," said the pastor. "But I also knew the husband's statement was pretty accurate. I'd preached so strongly that parents are to 'raise their children in the fear and admonition of the Lord' that parents who felt they didn't measure up couldn't even ask for help."

Counselor and former pastor Jim Conway observes, "Most people only know their pastor through the pulpit. I don't think some pastors perceive how seriously people take them, and how powerful their images are."

To compensate for this image, many pastors are careful in their use of illustrations. Authoritarian pastors, when talking about problems, generally use illustrations outside of themselves — illustrating *other people's* problems, never their own.

Haddon Robinson, president of Denver Seminary and a teacher of preachers, says, "Sometimes preachers stand on the side of God and speak his words to the people, but it's just as important to stand with the people and articulate their situation to God."

Many preachers try to balance their presentations, speaking *to* the people as well as speaking *for* the people. They find a place for "Thus saith the Lord" as well as place for "Woe is me, for I am a man of unclean lips."

For instance, the subject of adultery can be preached simply, "Thou shalt not!" Or the point can be introduced: "It's not hard to see why people find themselves struggling with the temptation of adultery. When a chill sets in at home, when fatigue or stress or whatever causes you to sense a growing distance from your spouse, that's the moment we find ourselves wondering what it would be like to be married to someone else. Then, it seems, it's not long before you meet someone who listens, who laughs at the old jokes your spouse endures in silence, who makes you feel *alive* again. And you begin to think, *What could be so wrong in spending some time with someone who makes me feel so good?* Anyone who's been married more than a year has probably had at least fleeting thoughts like this. But what do these thoughts, if pursued, bring as a result? Why is it that God says, 'Thou shalt not?' . . ."

Another pastor said, "I try to be empathetic from the pulpit, to let people know 'I am for you. There's a reason you are experiencing what you are experiencing, and I'd like to help reduce that pain. I am not in the job of inducing guilt; that's the Holy Spirit's task. I'm not God. My task is to help you understand where you are and help you to move toward where you truly want to be.' As I put myself in that role and talk about my own struggles, people see me as a possible source of help for them."

At the same time, pastors do point out that help is available, that things can be different, thanks to the resources God provides for his people.

R. Lofton Hudson tells the story of a textile factory where this sign hangs over each machine: "If your thread gets tangled, send for the foreman." A new employee went to work, and soon her threads were tangled, but she tried to untangle them herself. The more she tried, the worse they became. Finally, in desperation, she called for help.

"Why didn't you call for me sooner?" the foreman asked.

"I did my best," she replied in self-defense.

"Doing your best," he answered with a smile, "is sending for me."

Preaching is one of the important elements of climate control. And when used wisely, along with the other tools, it can produce an atmosphere where people are more apt to ask for help and accept it when it is offered.

---

1. Eugene H. Peterson. *Five Smooth Stones for Pastoral Work.* (Atlanta: John Knox, 1980) p. 110.

FIVE

INSTILLING A DESIRE TO CHANGE

Totally without hope one cannot live. To live without hope is to cease to live. Hell is hopelessness. It is no accident that above the entrance to Dante's hell is the inscription: "Leave behind all hope, you who enter here."

FYODOR DOSTOYEVSKY

Katie, a thirty-five-year-old mother of two, first came to Pastor Frank Garrett to ask his help with her failing marriage. Her husband, Clark, had never been a churchgoer, and he resented Katie's involvement. They had married young; Katie had known Clark was not a Christian, and to marry him she defied her parents' wishes. Now Clark was refusing to let her bring the kids to church and ridiculing her mealtime prayers.

Pastor Frank tried to contact Clark, and Katie tried to get him to come for joint counseling, but he refused "to see any preachers." Eventually Clark walked out on the marriage and filed for divorce.

Strangely, however, this story is not about Clark's refusal to accept help. It's about Katie's.

Within three months of the divorce being finalized, Katie was engaged to another man — an acquaintance from work, who also never attended church and, as far as Frank could tell, had never made any sort of spiritual commitment.

When some of her friends began suggesting it was too soon to be dating again, let alone remarry, Katie began withdrawing from her church friends. When Frank phoned her, she seemed curt. He asked, "How is your relationship with Will any different from your relationship with Clark?"

"You just don't understand how tough it is to be a single parent," Katie told him. "I need a man in my life. My kids need a father."

She would not change her mind. She and Will got married in a civil ceremony, and Frank never saw Katie or her children again.

"She was getting into exactly the same situation. Everyone could see it but her," said Frank.

How do you help such people who have blinded themselves, who refuse to see? In the play *Faustus,* Goethe has the Devil introduce himself, "I am the spirit that denies" — an apt description of the spirit of self-deception within each of us.

Two reasons people often resist help are (1) they don't realize what they truly want out of life or (2) if they do, they don't believe they could ever achieve it. As a result, they ossify, forming patterns difficult to break.

If the first step in helping these people is creating an environment conducive to change, the next step is instilling a desire to change. When both the external and internal environments are realigned, real help is possible.

Here are some ways pastors have found to help individuals see the need for change.

Deep Desires, Not Deficiencies

One of the best ways to begin instilling a desire to change is to turn the conversation to the person's strengths.

"I don't approach people as if I'm the one with all the answers, as if I'm the doctor and they're sick. Instead, I begin by focusing where they're healthy. I want to find out what they are excited about," says Gary Gulbranson of Glen Ellyn (Illinois) Bible Church. He finds it helpful to work through a series of questions.

- What do you do well?
- What would you like out of life? What are your dreams? If

you were in control of the world, if you could really take the reins of your own life, where would you go with it?

- What do you think it would take to live that kind of life?
- Is what you're doing now heading you in that direction?

"Sometimes we don't even have to get past the first two questions before people wake up to their self-destructive behavior," he says. At times, people haven't faced the fact that the long-term results of their present behavior are not going to be what they want.

He used this approach while doing hospital visitation. He found himself talking with a college-age girl admitted for an eating disorder. As part of her therapy, she was supposed to go through a list of dissatisfactions in life and honestly evaluate how she felt about them.

When Gary asked what she was learning, she launched into the standard resentments: "I don't like my mom and dad. They put too much pressure on me to get good grades. My values aren't the same as my parents' — they're only concerned about making money. And they don't get along. I don't respect their relationship; that's why we have problems. They want me to get good grades because they're both really into education, and I don't get good grades, which makes them look bad to their friends."

Gary knew that tension with parental values is a normal part of growing up. It's certainly not enough to hospitalize someone with an eating disorder. But he let her air these surface issues. Then he simply got her to talk about herself.

"I appreciate the things you've shared," he said, "but I want to know who you are. You're an interesting person. You've told me a lot about who other people think you are. But who are you really? What do you like to do in your spare time, for instance?"

She mentioned reading murder mysteries. They discussed various mystery writers for a while.

"What else do you enjoy?"

"I like aerobics and exercise. Anything to make me sweat."

"Why is that important to you?"

She mentioned wanting to look good, but as she talked further, it eventually became clear that she was different than the other three members of her family. Her real problem was trying to change everyone else rather than recognizing the uniqueness of her own personality, accepting the differences, and fitting in.

Gary asked about her relationship with the church.

"My parents are religious, but I don't want to be like them."

"What kind of relationship with God would you like? How do you visualize God now?"

They talked for the next hour. "She really blossomed," Gary said later. "I can't say she immediately turned her life around, but we did break through that hard shell she'd put up." The key was starting with a healthy area and moving to goals and dreams before tackling the problems.

The idea of helping people articulate their goals and desires is especially effective in perhaps one of the most common dilemmas pastors face: handling wedding requests by couples with little or no spiritual commitment. Normally these couples want little more than to have a licensed member of the clergy fulfill a function. But most pastors recognize their deeper need for a spiritual foundation, even if the couple does not.

When Mark Bowman and Greta Holloway first walked into the church office, Kent Carlburg could tell they were angry. The way Mark, especially, sat on the edge of the chair, leaned forward, and glared at him, Kent felt like he was spoiling for a fight. When they'd called to set up an appointment with "a pastor," he figured they wanted someone to perform a wedding. He was right.

Mark growled, "We're getting married and need a preacher."

Kent tried to help them relax.

"Congratulations. I'm glad you're here. Tell me how you decided on me."

"Because the guy over at Heritage Church refused to marry us, but he said you might," Mark said.

Greta spoke up. "I used to go to Heritage when I was growing up, so we thought we'd be married there. But Reverend Morris refused to perform the ceremony unless we were members of the church. He said we were 'unequally yoked' — whatever that means. And he didn't approve of 'the way we handled our courtship,' which I don't consider any of his business. We thought it was a pastor's job to do weddings."

Kent made a mental note to ask Billy Morris at the next ministerial breakfast why he left the dirty work to him, but he grinned and said, "Tell me about yourselves. A wedding is a rather personal thing, and we preachers like to know whom we're working with."

Mark and Greta began to relax as they talked. Greta, it turned out, had made a commitment to Christ as a child but had stopped attending church during high school. Mark had never had any church experience. Neither had been married before.

"I'm not here to sit in judgment on you," Kent said. "You've decided to marry, and since there are no legal impediments I can see, you have every right to do so. But tell me, why do you want to be married in a church? Why not a civil ceremony?"

Mark and Greta looked blankly at one another. Kent let the silence linger. Finally Greta said, "I guess we want God's blessing on our marriage."

"What does God's blessing mean to you?"

"Well, uh, I guess it means he'll help things go smoother."

"God's blessing is a very important thing to seek," said Kent. "I'm glad it's important to you. How do you think you get God's blessing?"

"I suppose by, you know, following his rules."

"Have you been following them?"

"Well, no."

"But you really want God's blessing," repeated Kent. "Why is that important to you in the days ahead?"

As they talked, both Mark and Greta admitted they were somewhat insecure about entering marriage, in fact even their present relationship — they were living together — was a result of their feeling alone and insecure. "We felt we needed to know each other," Mark said.

Kent pointed out that part of God's blessing is his protection and security when facing uncertain days. "The way to be certain of God's blessing — and to know the security of belonging to him — is to become part of his family."

Over the next several weeks, as Kent continued to meet with them, Mark decided to commit himself to Christ, and Greta reaffirmed her previous commitment. They have since joined the church and attend regularly.

The turning point from their anger and defensiveness to an openness to the gospel came as a result of the pastor pointing not to their deficiency but to their previously unarticulated desire.

Rebuilt Hope

The second reason people often resist help is because they truly do not believe any better way is possible. They've lost hope and therefore the desire to try.

As Jurgen Moltmann writes: "Men die when they are suddenly struck with the impression that everything is without prospect for them. They simply give up, even if there are no physical causes for their death. Others become criminals out of hopelessness. One young burglar in Berlin related that he had sought a job at different places but was again and again thrown out. 'And then came the point where nothing made any difference to me.' This is typical. He became a criminal because his hope in life had turned into self-hate and he had given up on himself."

Pastors most often see this phenomenon in people who complain, "Nothing can be done anymore. If we'd done something fifteen years ago, maybe things could be different, but not now." Perhaps bankruptcy looms. Perhaps the marriage is crumbling or opportunities are lost. The problem lies deeper than not wanting help; it's doubting that any help is possible.

Maybe they weren't aware enough when the problem was younger and could have been dealt with, and now, by the time they're really in pain, they assume the situation is hopeless. Perhaps they have already tried inferior solutions that offered the appearance of relief — a husband chasing another woman or a mother leaving the family to pursue two jobs and aerobics.

With these providing a temporary outlet to their pain, they do not want to attempt the massive reconstruction on their marriage, the real problem. They don't see any hope for marital improvement. Often the turning point for embattled spouses is actually believing things can get better.

Counselor Robert J. Carlson has found an important element in the recovery of hope: He brings hopeless couples together and introduces them to couples whose marriages were once in serious trouble. These couples simply tell their survival stories. They describe how they returned from the brink of divorce.

He reports the response of Dawn, a woman ready to give up. After meeting with three other couples whose marriages were founded in hope, tested in disillusionment, shaken by pain and misunderstanding, and rebuilt through a long, significant process, Dawn said: "You know, we've got a lot of problems. Our families are a mess. All of Bob's brothers and sisters are divorced. His father has been married three times and now has taken a male lover. My father abused me, and my mother hated me. I know Bob and I have been terribly cruel to each other, but when I heard today what those couples have been through, I believe we can make this marriage work, too. I don't know yet how to go about it, but I believe we can find a way. I'd like to tell you what I think some of our problems are. Maybe you can help us with them."

This kind of response is not unusual, according to Carlson. "To hear someone else speak about the unspeakable — personal failure of a marriage contract, the death of dreams, the despair and pain — yet with a message of hope is a powerful encouragement. Again and again, I've seen couples find they can begin to believe in the possibilities of the future. That's what hope is about. It's the necessary ingredient for people to do the hard work necessary to rebuild."[1]

Hope Blended with Realism

As important as hope is, it must be not be offered apart from the reality of the situation, with all its seemingly hopeless elements. A snappy "Don't give up . . . things will work out . . . believe me" rings hollow unless the pastor or counselor clearly communicates that he understands the depth of the problem.

Perhaps this can best be illustrated by the story of one young husband who didn't particularly want help with his crumbling marriage. It shows how one pastor broke through the barriers — after others had failed.

Jed Rauch prided himself on being able to take care of himself. He was raised on a farm and learned from his father that work had to be done whether you felt like it or not. In high school, Jed earned a black belt in karate, which led to a lot of self-confidence, which extended even to his spiritual life.

"I was so macho I remember praying, 'Lord, if you ever need someone to take on the Devil, here I am, ready to go one on one with him,' " Jed admits.

Yet Jed had a quiet side. Hours in the fields had taught him to enjoy moments of solitude. "There's nothing I enjoy quite as much as sitting alone on the tractor watching the sun go down."

His most vivid memory from growing up took place while driving the tractor through a weedy slough on the twenty acres farthest from the house.

"The sun was going down between two clouds in an otherwise clear sky," he recalls. "I was watching the sun set as I brought the tractor into a turn, and suddenly, a pheasant took to flight just to my left, and before it could clear the weeds, I saw a fox leap up, pick it out of the air, and begin dragging it across the field. I followed at a comfortable distance just to see what the fox was going to do. When she got near the creek, I shut the tractor down to watch. The fox dragged the pheasant to her den, and I saw three pups have dinner while the mother just sat and watched."

After that Jed considered the field animals almost friends.

"I began to notice the fox pups would chase the implements I was pulling with the tractor. But if I shut down the machine to get a better look, they'd run and hide. I also began to notice nests that killdeer had built in the middle of the field. Stupid birds. I guess they figured no animal would look for prey in an open field. But they forgot about tractors. I'd be driving when suddenly I'd hear the squawk of the mother, even above the noise of the tractor. Then I'd see her trying to lure me away from the nest with her broken wing act. But I'd find the nest and move it to part of the field I'd already worked. The mother would always come back to it! I guess I learned you don't have to always be 'doing something' to enjoy life."

Shortly after high school, Jed met Sandy, a hair stylist, while getting a haircut. She had recently moved to the town from Chicago. Jed was attracted by her vivacious personality; she seemed to enjoy talking with everyone and made friends quickly. In turn, Sandy was attracted to the strong young farmer who could also talk about birds and sunsets. Before long, they were dating, engaged, and within a year, married.

The very qualities that attracted them to each other, however, soon became the source of severe problems in their marriage. Jed was a hard worker, but after he started his own trucking business, his work began to consume him.

"I knew the proper priorities were God first, family second, and work third," says Jed, "but if I would have been honest, I'd have had to admit my priorities were work first, work second, and work third."

After a day of work, Jed would sit outside, stare at the sunset, and ponder his work problems. If Sandy, who was eager to talk to her husband or get together with friends, tried to strike up a conversation, Jed would tell her to leave him alone.

Within a couple years, after the birth of their daughter Adelle, Jed found both his business and marriage floundering. A number of accidents and breakdowns with his trucks left him with huge debts. More and more arguments were erupting with Sandy, and while Jed prided himself on "winning" the arguments, he also saw his relationship with Sandy deteriorating. But he didn't want anyone's help with either the business or the marriage.

"Asking for help is humiliating," he explained later. "For someone raised to take care of himself, asking for help is an admission of failure. I wasn't ready to do that.

"After Sandy's repeated requests, we finally did try to get counseling. But it was a bad experience. We first went to the pastor at our church, and we liked him, but he was so busy, he couldn't see us more than once a month. That wasn't enough, so he referred us to a counselor at a pastoral counseling center. But the eight sessions were worthless as far as I was concerned. My attitude was bad to start with, and the guy didn't tell us anything we didn't already know. He tried to get me to 'share my feelings.' It was hard for me to say honestly how I felt toward Sandy. I didn't know. I'm not used to talking about feelings."

Jed also felt the counselor tried to pigeon-hole them into a certain problem category.

"When he said, 'Well, 53 percent of people with marriage problems have the same situation you two do,' I knew the guy was a jerk. He didn't know us well enough to generalize about our situation. I decided I wasn't going to be honest with him. I manipulated the rest of the sessions for my own advantage — using them as bargaining chips with Sandy, so I could say 'I'm doing what you want.'

"Sandy took the counseling seriously, but I didn't. The counselor kept talking about 'spending more time together.' He said we should 'go to the zoo,' or do things together at home. I said, 'We do! We spent all last Saturday planting flowers together.' It was a slight exaggeration — Sandy had worked in front and I was in the back yard, but I was playing games with the counselor because I knew our problems were deeper than lack of time together. I decided I wasn't going to open up until I found somebody worth opening up to, and this clown wasn't. If we had problems, they were things we were just going to have to work out."

Unfortunately, they couldn't "work things out," and their relationship became increasingly strained. The business also continued to crumble as more trucks and trailers were disabled. He had a hard time finding good drivers. With more downtime, the debts skyrocketed. Jed called his lawyer to investigate bankruptcy procedures.

He began to fantasize about jumping in his pickup truck, driving to the mountains and living alone, supporting himself with day labor.

Suddenly he began to realize he had a choice to make. Up until now, he had basically drifted along in life. "I felt like I was living my life and God was in my hip pocket — always there, but not someone I had to take seriously. Now I knew I had a decision to make — to stay and try to work things out, or to bail out.

"I have to admit, when Sandy said, 'We are going to get a divorce unless something changes around here,' I wasn't surprised or particularly concerned. I was sort of numb. The idea of divorce actually sounded attractive because at least I'd have my peace and quiet again. But at the same time, I'm big on commitments. When I make a promise, I pride myself on keeping it, and I didn't want to be the one responsible for the marriage falling apart."

One of Jed's high school friends, Eric, knew about their marital difficulties. Eric attended another church in town and kept telling Jed, "Our pastor is an excellent counselor. Why don't you give him a try?" Sandy, of course, knew he wasn't cooperating with the other counselor and was willing to try anyone.

"After six weeks of Eric talking about Pastor Barry, I gave in," says Jed. "Sandy and I went to the Sunday services, and I was impressed enough that Barry seemed like an intelligent but real human being that we made an appointment to see him."

The counseling approach with Pastor Barry was completely different from their previous experience.

They found Barry easy to talk to, and unlike the previous counselor, he didn't say, "I know what your problem is, and I know what you have to do to fix it." He took a hard, honest approach.

"What really impressed me," said Jed, "was at the end of our first meeting, Barry said, 'I can't say whether you two should stay together or get a divorce. We'll have to see.' *This is a pastor talking?* I thought. *And he doesn't know if we should stay together or not?* I'd been sure he was going to tell us to stay together or else, but he didn't have that attitude. He let us know that either way, *we* had to make the decision — and live with the consequences."

Suddenly Jed realized he was responsible for the relationship. It had a chilling effect. *Finally, here's a guy who's being realistic,* he said to himself.

"Barry said, 'You've got serious problems in this marriage. I don't know if we'll be able to work them out, but I'll try if you will. And we'll ask God to help heal this relationship. I'd like to meet with you for as long as it takes.' He didn't put a time limit on it, which I liked."

In subsequent sessions, Barry explained how he felt about divorce and its consequences, but he continued to say, "but how I feel is not as important as the decision you have to make."

"Instead of telling us to 'take trips to the zoo and everything will work out,' he got us to work on the fundamentals: learning to love again, praying for one another, including God in our relationship, doing acts of kindness."

He also covered specific problem areas. "He pointed out that Sandy needed to back off when I first came home from work, to give me some time alone," said Jed. "But he also told me I couldn't stay in a coma all evening. I had to begin to open up, too. He made sense. He gave us an exercise: The first thing we said to each other after I came home at night had to be positive, something good that had happened that day or something we appreciated about each other."

The relationship between Jed and Sandy is still not without tension. Jed's business is exhausting and demands much time away from home. He and Sandy are still learning to communicate without being accusing. But after two years, they are still together, and they're still working at it. For them, the key was a pastor who took their problem as seriously as they did.

A Long-Term Process

Through the power of suggestion, pleading, or coercion, a person's behavior can be changed for short periods of time. But long-term results rarely happen as a result of one sermon or a single confrontation.

Not only do people want quick solutions, sometimes the counselors do, too. As one pastor said, "After you have the couple hug each other and pray, and they leave, and then they come back a week later with the same problem, what do you do? Tell them to hug and pray again?"

There is a temptation to give up. "I can sympathize with my colleagues who recommend divorce, even though I strongly disagree with them," said a Christian counselor. "When you keep meeting with someone who has a problem that seems immovable, and the person's been acting this way for three months, it seems like forever. So to help stabilize the person, you say 'Go ahead, get the divorce' because it seems like the way to ease the pain. But unfortunately, it is only the beginning of woes."

Long-term change happens over time as God works. The key for the pastor is to look for God's subtle activity, to highlight it, to bring it to consciousness and affirm it. It means asking, "What is God doing with you?" It's a process of helping resistant people discover the reasons they are in their present situation, then convincing them things can be better, and then training them in a new way of life. This process usually takes years, not months.

"People can learn a lot in a short time, but to actually implement it, to make it functional, may take years," said a Wisconsin pastor. "When people have spent five or twenty-five years learning bad habits, they can't unlearn those and learn other habits overnight. Skills take time to perfect. I tell struggling couples that we're talking about a four-year process of learning to relate again. It's not unlike a college education."

It requires — and devours — time.

In the meantime, the job of the minister is to keep the channels open — and, since hidden factors are often at work, to make sure the real issues have been identified.

---

1. Robert J. Carlson. "Hope for Hurting Marriages," *Leadership*, vol. 7, no. 1 (Winter 1986), pp. 34–35.

SIX

UNCOVERING HIDDEN AGENDAS

*Our Lord finds our desires, not too
strong, but too weak. We are half-hearted
creatures, fooling about with drink and
sex and ambition when infinite joy is
offered us, like an ignorant child who
wants to go on making mud pies in a
slum because he cannot imagine what is
meant by the offer of a holiday at the sea.
We are far too easily pleased.*

C. S. LEWIS

As anyone who has counseled knows, when people do ask for help, it is usually not in the area of their real need. They rarely mention their real source of pain without first sending up one or more trial balloons — the presenting problems.

The way these "safe" issues are handled determines whether they will reveal the underlying hurt.

"Any time a person comes for counseling, I assume the topic of discussion is not the real issue," said one pastor who's made counseling his specialty. "But the surface issue has to be dealt with. There may be pride on the surface, for instance, and a huge hurt underneath. When you try to see why the pride is there, often it's because the person doesn't want to admit the hurt. Anger on the surface often camouflages an underlying fear. Recognizing that is important."

These camouflaged souls represent a special category of people who need help: those hiding their need — either consciously or unconsciously. In order to help those who don't want help, we must recognize that some of these people *will* ask for help, but they will ask for it through a tangential issue.

One woman made a point several Sundays in a row to

shake hands with the pastor at the door after the service.

"She would take my hand and look me in the eye in such a way that I knew she wanted to say something, but with other people around, she didn't get it said," the pastor noticed.

Finally one Sunday she asked, "Can I have an appointment?"

"Of course. Any time. Just call the office and set one up."

She came in that week. She was a long-time church attender, and she and her husband had raised three sons. They were happy, as far as the pastor knew. But when she came in, she started to cry.

"Go ahead and cry," the pastor said, "But I'd like to know what it is that's hurting."

After a minute or two she said, "I'm afraid to die."

"Are you ill?"

"No. I'm very well. But I'm afraid to die."

"Why?"

"I know I'm saved. I know I'm going to heaven. But I'm afraid to die."

The pastor suspected something more was involved, but he addressed the immediate issue. "We all are somewhat afraid. Death is something we haven't experienced, and anything unknown and alien like that, we dread."

"No," she said. "I'm afraid. I'm guilty."

"Guilty of what?"

"I've never told anybody," she said. "My sons would die if they knew. My husband has never known."

She paused. The pastor silently waited. Finally she spoke.

"When I was twelve years old, I let a neighbor man play with me. He just used his hands, but he played with me. I felt so dirty. I never told my mother. I never told anybody."

"How did you get along all these years?" the pastor asked.

"I forgot it. It was a girlhood mistake, and I just plain forgot it. I was so busy loving my husband and raising my sons. I've had a wonderful life, and I enjoy the church, but now the boys are grown and my husband is gone a great deal, and when I'm alone, all the memories come back. I can't sleep nights. I'm seeing things that aren't there. I'm hearing voices. I'm scared to die, and yet I know I'm going to."

The pastor slowly asked, "Do you believe what you did back then was sinful?"

"Oh, yes," she said. "No question about it."

"Well, how did you treat every other sin in your life?"

"I simply asked God to forgive me."

"Did you ask God to forgive you for this?"

"I've never been able to."

"Would you like me to help you?"

"Please."

The two of them knelt in the office, and right there, she broke down and asked God to please forgive her for an action that took place forty years earlier. When they were done, she said, "Should I tell my husband?"

"Why?" asked the pastor. "He wouldn't think any less of you — you know he adores you — but he hasn't known for all these years. It wouldn't do him any good to know. It's forgiven. What God forgives he wipes out. It's gone."

The next Sunday when she came by to shake hands, she took hold of the pastor's hand, looked up, and said, "It's wonderful not to be afraid."

The people standing around hadn't the foggiest notion of what she was talking about. But she was free.

Issues that deeply hidden don't usually just pop to the surface. The pastor certainly would not have had any way of ferreting out that problem. It was only her confidence in the pastor — she'd studied him for several weeks and seen how he'd handled her question about death — that allowed her to reveal her inner pain.

Signs of a Deeper Issue

The consistent pastoral presence and the ability to be slow to speak and quick to listen will help uncover most hidden agendas, but certain clues help pastors minister more effectively in these situations.

1. Some statements give it away, such as "Pastor, you never need call on me. I'm well cared for. You just spend your time calling on people who have real needs."

"I discovered that's some people's way of saying, 'Please pay attention to me — I'm in need.' It took me years to learn that," mused a pastor from Los Angeles. "Often they've got unresolved problems they would love to talk about, but they're afraid. They will want to argue with you over some fine point of doctrine or procedure or share a bad experience in the church. But when you get beneath it all, you find they've got a desperate loneliness, or their prayer life is delinquent, or they're not sure of their salvation."

2. Inappropriate emotion is another clue of an untapped hurt. One pastor from Kansas City, Earl Jenkins, met a young couple visiting the church for the first time. Their first words after introducing themselves were "We've been to three churches since moving here from New York City six weeks ago, and this is the first one that hasn't completely disgusted us."

Earl gulped but said half-jokingly, "I hope we don't step out of line." Then he introduced them to a young couple from the church and was pleased to see them easily strike up a conversation.

The next week, they again attended both Sunday school and the worship service, so Earl arranged to visit them. As soon as he sat down, he was facing two Grand Inquisitors.

"Why are churches so formal? I don't see any such institutionalism in the New Testament," said the young man with surprising emotion.

"Your church is like all the others. It's locked into a constitution. Where's the Spirit? Where's the life?" demanded the young woman.

Earl refused to take the bait. He breathed a quick, silent prayer for patience and a nondefensive spirit. "It's interesting to hear that," he said. "You've been here two weeks. I've been here eight years. I'm sure I miss things that are right in front of my nose. Tell me what you observed."

They mentioned the classical hymns, the readings, the sobriety and formal structure of the service.

"Accurate observations," said Earl. "We do believe the

Spirit can be present in structure as well as spontaneity. But you saw what we were the first week. What brought you back the second week?"

"Well, some of the people did seem to care about us."

"It's tough to uproot yourselves and relocate half a continent away, isn't it?" said Earl. Was this the hurt that made them so pugnacious?

As they admitted their sense of loss over leaving relatives and friends on the East Coast, Earl began to sense a thaw. Before he left, the couple had warmed considerably. The next Sunday, they came back. Two Sundays later, they were ready to become members. Never again did Earl hear anything about formal institutionalism. Instead, the couple eventually shared with their Sunday school class how grateful they were for a church that welcomed them into the family.

"I was glad I let them ventilate without responding directly," Earl concluded. "If you assume an angry person is hurting, you'll be right 90 percent of the time. And if you can identify the hurt, even indirectly, and offer some comfort, often you've turned the enemy into a friend."

3. When the complaints are scattered and seemingly disconnected, or when they're only about recent events, that's another indication a deeper, unseen stream is flowing.

Jim and Valsa had been married eighteen months. He was twenty-three and worked nights at a bakery. She was thirty-five. They had a son three months old. They'd told their pastor, Calvin Thulman, that they were struggling with some things in their relationship but never mentioned anything specific.

Then one night Valsa called in tears. "Pastor, Jim's gone! He walked out. He may be staying with some friends across town. I'm not sure."

"Is he coming back?"

"I don't know. He just left in a huff." Valsa explained that Jim kept coming home late, and she suspected him of immorality. She had accused him. He angrily denied it. And things escalated until she threw a colander at him. He said, "I don't have to put up with this!" and stormed out of the house.

"I know I'm part of the problem," said Valsa. "But what should I do?"

"Well, Valsa, let's begin by praying." Calvin said a prayer over the phone. He agreed to call Jim at work that night and try to set up a meeting with both of them.

When Calvin called, Jim agreed to meet, though he said, "Valsa has just become so demanding, so jealous. She thinks there's something wrong all the time. There's nothing wrong with our marriage — we've got a kid, don't we?"

The next night, the three of them met in Calvin's office. He asked each of them what they felt the pinch points were in their marriage.

Valsa began, "I can't trust him. He goes and delivers donuts to the girls' dorm at the university. And he never tells me how long he stays in there! He never tells me what he does."

"I delivered ten dozen sweet rolls," said Jim. "It's the truth!"

"I'll bet it's the truth," she said sarcastically. "Besides that, you won't fix up the house. I hate the colors in the kitchen, and two weeks ago I bought wallpaper, and you still haven't put it up. Last week I fixed breakfast for you when you got home, but you said you were too tired to talk and went to bed."

Jim countered, "When I do want to talk, all you do is complain. You complain about the colors. You complain about where we live. I can't do anything to please you."

How in the world can you fight tooth and nail over petty things that have come up in the last two weeks? thought Calvin. Such scattered complaints about such recent offenses signaled Calvin that they weren't touching the real injury. There were too many charges and not one of them was really heartfelt. He sensed they were flinging accusations out of frustration. The underlying problem had to be something that had been building for a while.

Calvin probed, "I know your work schedule is tough, Jim. It has been ever since you were married. But how much time a day do you spend together?"

They both looked rather blank. Calvin pressed on. "Do you eat meals together? Are you sleeping in the same bed together? When was the last time just the two of you did something together?"

Their mouths dropped slack. "We're not together much. Valsa sleeps at night, and I sleep during the daytime," said Jim.

"He gets home at 9 A.M. and sleeps until supper time," Valsa added. "We usually eat an evening meal before he heads off to work at 10 P.M."

"Is it possible that much of your frustration comes from your work schedule? You're not sleeping together. I don't mean just sexually. Even physically, you're not next to each other. There's no time for renewal."

"I've had this job for four years," said Jim. "I've applied other places, but the only openings would have meant a cut in pay."

Calvin said. "I want to meet again next week. But let me give you some homework. Would you both pray — just pray — about whether this job situation is the key element in this problem?"

They agreed and set up another appointment for the following Wednesday.

That Saturday, Jim called Calvin. "You're right. I think the job is the real problem, not all those other things we were talking about. And you won't believe it! I just got a call from the manager at the Blue Coach Restaurant. I had talked with him about a job a year ago, but nothing was available. But now he needs an assistant manager. I can work days — and without a pay cut! I'm going to take it."

Calvin continued to meet with Jim and Valsa to work on their communication patterns, but it was clear the biggest hurdle had been overcome. Calvin rejoices in both the answer to prayer and that he was right about the underlying issue.

Uncovering the Need

In addition to simply providing a consistent, trustworthy pastoral presence and suggesting possible problem areas, one pastor has discovered that prayer can provide an atmosphere where people feel free to reveal the deeper issues.

"Many times I'll take the person's hand and we'll pray," says Ken Leone of Spirit of Christ Church in Denver. "We'll pray about the issues we've talked about, and then I trust the Lord to speak through me. Perhaps — and I'm careful not to be manipulative — I'll softly interrupt my prayer and say 'I sense that you're terribly frustrated. Is there anything else? Is there something way down deep that maybe we can ask Jesus to help you with?'

"Or perhaps I'll say 'I'm sensing, just from holding your hands, that there's an anger here. Is there something you really need to talk about yet?' Many times in the context of the prayer they will suddenly start to cry and then it all comes out."

An eighteen-year-old boy came to see his pastor because he was wondering whether he should take martial arts classes. He wanted to learn karate, but as he told the pastor, "I've seen some black candles in the instructor's home, and I don't want to get involved in any satanic worship or anything that's going to harm my Christian walk."

After discussing it, they prayed, and the pastor said, "Lord, help Ted know what to do. But even more importantly, help him know why he's doing it. Help him to use these skills to honor you, not just to have power over others."

Suddenly Ted shivered and began crying uncontrollably. The pastor put an arm around his shoulders and waited. Slowly the sobs subsided and Ted blurted out a devastating memory.

"You know my dad was killed in a plane crash three years ago. Two weeks before he died, I found out I had been cut from the high school football team. And Dad was disappointed. He'd worked with me on tackling and being tough, but I wasn't tough enough. When I told him I was cut, he said, 'Geez, I have a wimp for a son.' " Ted began sobbing again.

His pain had been so repressed that only the prayerful atmosphere and the pastor's putting the shame into words allowed the real issue to come out — not martial arts — but whether he would ever be able to please a dead father.

"Once that came out," reports the pastor. "It was like releasing a pressure cooker. He became calm and peaceful and was able to look at the real issue and deal with it. But I suspect when he first came to see me, he honestly didn't know what the real issue was."

It came out through prayer, through accepting the original proposition at face value, but also recognizing that there might be more underneath the surface.

The camouflage hiding the real issues often slows the process of helping these people, but it need not prevent the healing. Many times the catalyst for restoring wholeness is an effective use of indirect confrontation.

SEVEN

CONFRONTING INDIRECTLY

Whom you would change, you must first love.

MARTIN LUTHER KING, JR.

One of the interesting discoveries of the Apollo space program was that somewhere between earth and the moon, the spaceship reaches a point where the moon's gravitational effect is greater than the earth's. The spacecraft is literally falling *away* from earth. The only way it will ever return to earth is to fire its engine to escape the moon's gravitational pull.

People, like spaceships, will also sometimes drift past the point of natural return. "You can almost feel it," said one counselor. "I would say more than half the people who come for counseling have already passed that point."

There seems to be a point where the person begins to act as if *I'm going to do it my way no matter what anyone says. If you get right down to it, I'm going to do what I want even if God disapproves. I don't care.*

What are some of the engine bursts needed to break the outward drift and propel people homeward? At this point, atmosphere alone is insufficient. Some kind of confrontation is needed — either direct or indirect. Since the indirect approach is easier on the adrenal glands, let's start there.

The Necessary Foundation

The first step is to develop a relationship with the person that he or she values. Without a relational base, prompting change proves difficult.

Often pastors pick up rumblings of problems from a third party who doesn't know if the claim is true or not. What to do? Become a detective? Ignore it until the person himself eventually decides to see you?

Most pastors begin by trying to establish or strengthen their personal relationship with the individual in question.

"I don't go around checking the validity of the story. But I do let the person know I care about him or her, and in the process, often the situation comes tumbling out. It happened just last month," said a Baptist pastor in the South.

"I'd heard that a man in our church had violent outbursts with his wife. At times she feared for her life. He's a dentist, so I just showed up unannounced and sat on a stool in his office until he finished with a patient. He came in and said, 'What are you doing here?'

"I said, 'I just want to pray with you, Fred. I try to visit everyone periodically. I know you're facing some struggles, and I care for you. Just let me have two minutes to pray with you.'

" 'OK,' he said. He had patients waiting, but he paused, we prayed, and I kept it to two minutes. He didn't say much other than that he appreciated me stopping by. But three days later, he was in *my* office saying, 'OK, now let me tell you what's happening.' I didn't have to ask him."

A relationship functions as the prime mover in producing change. Preaching and congregational services can help create an atmosphere conducive to change and instill a desire for something better, but the work of actual change usually demands more than a conducive atmosphere.

"I've found people don't change attitudes or patterns of behavior on Sunday morning," said the pastor of a community church. "Change happens when they see how it works in somebody else's life. They can't just hear about it; they have to see it. That's what makes our small-group ministries so important. Talking about 'How I handled a problem in my job this week' shows others how the Christian life is lived."

The function of a preaching service is primarily to display, almost like an advertisement, that "A better way is available." But for more information, people want to see it fleshed out. Making significant life changes demands a relationship of trust.

Most of us don't trust people who have an obvious agenda for us. We feel we are being manipulated for some ulterior motive. For pastors, part of this means letting the individual know you can be trusted not to reveal his problems to other people. "I try to let them see that I care about them and have *their* best interests in mind, not my own," said one rural minister. In most cases, the key is to find or develop common interests. This is especially true of people who have little involvement in the church.

In such cases, "I've learned not to talk about my agenda but about their agenda," said an Ohio pastor. He began meeting with two unchurched friends for pizza on Sunday evenings after the church service. "For over a year we talked about nothing but the price of cattle, cultivation techniques, and life around the farm. But as a result, we began to find other common interests — fishing and backpacking. Eventually they began attending church and made commitments to Christ."

Others Who Can Get Through

Now most pastors admit they can't find common ground with everyone. Perhaps this is one way of selecting people to try to help personally. When no common ground appears, perhaps other Christians who speak the same language can be brought in.

We normally think of doing this with literal languages. One pastor met a medical doctor from Pakistan who had become a Christian. The pastor introduced the doctor to a missionary friend who had served in Pakistan, and the doctor was very impressed that the missionary was able to speak such fluent Pakistani. As a result, he invited many of his non-Christian friends to his home for a dinner party and also invited the missionary to come and present his testimony in Pakistani. The dinner and gospel presentation were very well received. The pastor initiated that contact because he saw the importance of putting people together who speak the same language.

But this pastor has also done the same thing with people who speak the language of motorcycles.

"I saw a group of young men who were drifting away from church life," he said. "I noticed they all rode motorcycles. Since several of our solid young men were bikers, too, I encouraged them to get together. Before long we'd started a group of motorcycle buffs called the Retreads. I specifically invited people from the church who had an interest in motorbikes to get together, and out of this common ground, relationships were built with these fringe people."

Other pastors have used such interests as hunting, fishing, backpacking, woodworking, or photography to build relationships with those who won't acknowledge their need.

Another way to help people who need help but won't ask for it is to point out that there are others like them in the church.

"One man came to me, very embarrassed, and confessed that his teenage son had a drinking problem," said a minister in the Church of the Brethren. "I realized the problem was probably as much the father's as it was the son's, but the father wouldn't admit it. He told me, 'Please keep this confidential because the church wouldn't understand.' "

The minister said, "I'm wondering, would you be interested in meeting with some other people in the church who are in this exact same situation? If I got their permission, would you talk with them? I think it would be helpful for all of you."

The man refused — at first. "I've found there's reluctance initially," observed the minister, "because they doubt whether it's really so. There's a certain amount of pride that comes from thinking *My problem is so bad, nobody else has had it as bad as I've got it*. It's a sick self-concept, but it's real. These people seem to think, *I make the pastor worry about me because he's never seen anyone like me before. And, you know, God owes me something because he's given me these special problems. No one's ever endured my unique situation*."

Eventually, however, the father did meet with others and gradually began owning up to his own struggle with alcohol.

"When I give the name of the person they should talk to, invariably the initial reaction is 'Jack Edwards? He seems so together! I didn't know he'd been through anything like this!' But when they get together, there's a tremendous empathy that develops. It's one of the most effective ways of getting through."

Other churches do this with anyone remarrying after a divorce. Many times, people marrying for the second time do not want help. They feel, rightly or wrongly, that they are looked down on, persecuted. They are rarely open to counsel or caution about entering a new marriage. Several churches have tackled the problem by using other people from the church who have had similar experiences.

In one congregation, as part of the conditions to have the ceremony in the church, the couple agrees to a series of counseling sessions, and two or three of those sessions are with other people who have "blended families." The group acts as a barometer for the couple, helping them determine if they really are ready for marriage. If the wedding does take place, the group also provides a natural source of friends afterwards.

"They look for characteristics that indicate readiness to remarry," says the pastor. "Such things as a healthy admission of guilt for the failure of the previous marriage and a realistic acknowledgement of future problems. When these people say, 'You're just rebounding,' it communicates a lot stronger than if a pastor says it, because people who are divorced assume pastors will discourage remarriage."

It gets through because it comes from people who speak the same language.

Well-Placed Compliments

If the first "rocket burst" necessary to turn a life around is a relationship, either with you or others, the second might be a carefully worded comment offered in passing. Of the many ways to draw attention to a problem area, a sincere compliment is one of the most effective.

When you observe a couple getting stale with each other, the head-on approach — "I'm concerned about your relationship and I think you need to do something about it" — might not be well received.

Instead, one Christian counselor will say something like, "I love seeing the two of you together. You're really good for each other."

She's feeding that relationship, and at times, that's all it needs to perk up. Other times, it's a nonthreatening way to draw attention to a problem area.

"After I said that one time," the counselor reports, "the wife came up to me later and said, 'Things aren't as good as they seem.' It had opened up the issue."

The well-placed compliment lets them know you're observing their relationship but does so in a positive way.

Curiosity as an Ally

Yet another rocket engine is curiosity. Most people are curious, especially about themselves and their relationships. They generally are willing to consider *Maybe there's something I'm missing. What else is going on?* If pastors can provide glimpses of dynamics they don't see, people are often intrigued.

One pastor plays on curiosity by injecting questions that make people wonder whether or not they've seen the whole situation in its larger frame.

With one man so consumed by his career that his family was being neglected, his pastor invited him to lunch and asked, "John, if we asked your wife how cherished she feels, what do you think she would say?"

"What are you getting at?"

"Could you look me in the eye with a clean conscience and say, 'I know that I am making my wife feel absolutely loved and adored.' "

"No, but what's that got to do with it?"

The pastor considers that conversation the beginning of John's working on an area he'd never before considered a problem.

Yet another way of playing on curiosity is by sharing the stories of other people who have been in similar situations.

"One of the benefits of a long pastorate is that you develop a file of letters from past counselees," says David Seamands. "Some are from people whose stories did not end happily: *Against your advice, I married the man I told you about. In the beginning he said he would let me continue my involvement with the church, but gradually he got more and more jealous of the time I spent with my Christian friends. Now life with him is continual conflict. If other people come to see you contemplating remarriage to a nonbeliever, don't be afraid to be cruel. I wish you had convinced me I was making a mistake.*

"On the other hand, I have letters such as: *I broke up with the man I wanted to marry. Despite many tears at the time, I knew I had a duty to do what was right. In the years since, God has honored my obedience, and I met a fine Christian man who is a great father to my two boys.*

"I use these letters in my sermons and in my counseling to let people see that there is hope, that God can provide better solutions for their lives than they can themselves."

This kind of testimony can arouse curiosity in resistant individuals about how God might work in their situations.

Willingness to Be Used at Times

One pastor was counseling a bulemic who continually phoned him to confess that she had failed; once again she'd eaten too much and then forced herself to vomit.

"I felt I was being used," said the pastor. "She wasn't improving. She just wanted someone to hear her confession so she'd feel better. Normally I would have confronted her with my suspicion and refused to let the situation continue. But with this particular problem, I felt patience was the best approach because one of the key issues for bulemics is self-esteem. It would have been worse to reject her than it was to continue to offer the encouragement — even at the risk of being used."

That approach paid dividends later when the girl phoned to ask for help with another situation. She had been going to a secular counselor, who had instructed her to take off her clothes so he could caress her. He claimed she needed a parent figure — a role *he* was ready to provide.

"But he makes me uncomfortable," she told her pastor. "What should I do?" The pastor told her the counselor was wrong and that she should not go back to him. She did not. And saying no to the counselor greatly improved her self-respect.

"At that point," said the pastor, "I felt that all those hours on the phone listening to her confessions had been worthwhile. She felt she could trust me."

At times, of course, this means that we sometimes feel foolish, demeaned. But the long-term effects make the sacrifice worthwhile when the window of opportunity opens.

Jacques Maritain's book, *St. Thomas Aquinas*, recounts this attitude in the life of the Catholic scholar and saint: "One day a friar in a jovial mood cries out: 'Friar Thomas, come see the flying ox!' Friar Thomas goes over to the window. The other laughs. 'It is better,' the Saint says to him 'to believe that an ox can fly than to think that the religious can lie.' "

Friar Thomas — and we — may feel foolish in situations where people take advantage of us, but how much better to be used and eventually change a life than to be overly concerned about our need for independence, our mastery of situations.

Affirming the Importance of Life

Surprisingly, people tend to underestimate the value of their own lives. One of the duties of a pastor, especially when dealing with those destroying themselves but refusing help, is to remind people of the importance of life — their own included.

Remember the story of Samuel confronting Saul after Israel had defeated King Agag? Saul won a military victory but had violated God's commandment by allowing Agag and the best of his livestock to survive (1 Sam. 15). God's ways had been repudiated because Saul thought he knew better. The will of God was no longer the standard; Saul's will was. But Saul took charge without a sense of the spiritual powers at work.

When Samuel approached him, Saul said, "The Lord bless you! I have carried out the Lord's instructions."

"What then is this bleating of sheep in my ears?" Samuel responded.

When Samuel reviewed God's command, Saul insisted, "But I did obey the Lord. . . . I completely destroyed the Amalekites and brought back Agag their king. The soldiers took sheep and cattle from the plunder . . . in order to sacrifice them to the Lord your God."

It was a rationalization, which Harry Stack Sullivan once defined as "an exceedingly plausible but highly irrelevant" reason for one's behavior. At any rate, Samuel wasn't swallowing it.

His speech offers an interesting insight. "Though you are little in your own eyes, are you not the head of the tribes of Israel? The Lord anointed you king over Israel. And the Lord sent you on a mission. . . ."

Interestingly, he points out that Saul's sin was not thinking too highly of himself, but not thinking highly enough. He was unaware of the import of his actions. He underestimated the significance of the responsibility God had entrusted to him.

When it comes to helping those who don't want help, sometimes they, too, need to realize their own significance. God himself is interested in their decisions.

At times this can be done with indirect confrontation; at other times, however, it requires direct intervention.

E I G H T

CONFRONTING DIRECTLY

Whatever you do, let people see that you are in good earnest. You cannot break men's hearts by jesting with them or telling them a smooth tale or patching up a gaudy oration. Men will not cast away their dearest pleasures upon a drowsy request of one who seems not to mean as he speaks, or to care much whether his request is granted. Let us, therefore, rouse ourselves to the work of the Lord and speak to our people as for their lives.

RICHARD BAXTER

An elder, a close personal friend of the pastor, recently filed for corporate and personal bankruptcy. "It's a tragedy," said the pastor. "But he was a 'positive thinking' kind of person who, when you asked him how things were going, would always say, 'Fantastic!' That was part of the problem. He was so optimistic about his business that he didn't pay attention to the warning signs. Consequently, the business went under, and they're going to lose their house and most of their possessions. He finally told me about it *after* it happened."

"Fred," the pastor had said, "where have you been? I'm your friend. I'm your pastor. Why didn't you let me know sooner?"

"I don't know."

"Do you remember when you were at my house, and I talked about almost losing my first church because I hadn't yet learned how to read the financial accounts?"

"Yeah. You were asking about me then, weren't you?"

"Yes, I even asked about financial threats you faced in your business. Why wouldn't you tell me?"

"I just didn't want to admit defeat," said Fred.

Now he and the pastor are meeting regularly, talking through the financial and spiritual realities in all of this.

"Fred finally is ready to admit a need for help," the pastor says. "But his wife still won't talk to me. She's never rude, but when I call her once or twice a week, she always puts me off. I can help Fred, but I cannot help Naomi. And I grieve about that."

A month earlier, the pastor could not help Fred either. His indirect overtures had been rebuffed. At times, only direct intervention can break through, but for direct confrontation to be effective, timing is vitally important.

Signs of Readiness

When people finally become willing to work on an area of their life, pastors must know when the moment comes, and not jump the gun. What are some of the signs of openness?

One of them is *increased nervousness*, as evidenced by blushing, inability to sit still, or intestinal problems. Body language reveals much about a person's internal condition.

A second sign of readiness is *a lapse in the defensive posture*. Before a person is ready to deal with an issue, he usually will be defensive about it. "Initially, if someone is defensive, I'll overlook it and show acceptance," says psychiatrist Louis McBurney. "But after I've worked with him a while and feel we have more of a relationship, if he's still defensive, I might challenge him a bit — 'It sounds like you feel a little defensive about that subject.' I may still have to wait, but before long he'll usually say something like, 'You asked me about that before. What do you think about that issue?' Or something will indicate he's not reacting with the same degree of defensiveness, that he's feeling more secure. At that point, I can raise the issue directly."

Both of these principles were put into play by Pastor Daniel Frantz.

Daniel had been approached by Eddie Wiebe, a young man in the congregation. "Pastor, Sherry and I have been married only a year and a half, but we've got problems. She's still seeing an old boyfriend who works with her. They eat lunch together — just the two of them — twice a week."

"Have you two talked about the problem?"

"Yes, but she says she's not doing anything wrong. I say it may not be wrong, but it sure tears me up inside. When she won't end the contacts for me — for *us* — I wonder if she loves him more than me. Would you talk to her?"

"Does she know you're talking to me about this?"

"I told her we should consider counseling, but she says we shouldn't need counseling after only a year of marriage."

Daniel agreed to talk to Sherry, and as was his custom, he asked Eddie to perform a "familyectomy" — to take himself and their son out of the house so Daniel and his wife, Ruth, could talk to Sherry alone. He didn't want her to feel humiliated or emotionally pressured by any other family members. Eddie agreed that the next Tuesday night he would tell Sherry about 7 P.M. that he needed to pick up something at the hardware store. "Come back around eight," Daniel suggested.

The next Tuesday evening, with his wife along, Pastor Frantz rang the doorbell about 7:10. Sherry answered.

"Hello, Sherry. How are you?"

"Fine, Pastor. Hi, Ruth. Come in."

"First, let me tell you why we came," he said, planted on the porch. "We don't want to come in unless you really want us. Eddie told me you two have been struggling with some things. I'd like to talk about them, but I am not going to push myself in. I realize you didn't invite us to come here. I've come because as your friend and pastor, I felt I should. But we won't come in unless you invite us. If you say no we'll still be friends. We won't say anything more."

He paused and watched Sherry swallow hard. (He calls this his "Revelation 3:20 approach" because it makes sure the person knows her freedom was not being violated. But it also forces a decision.)

As is the case in most of Daniel's experiences, Sherry said, "Come in." They sat at the kitchen table.

"Eddie tells me he feels he's got some competition for you. I wanted to hear your side of things."

Sherry reassured Daniel that she wasn't doing anything wrong, that she and Roger were "just friends," that she had no guilt feelings, and that she was unafraid to be seen with Roger. As she continued to talk, however, Daniel noticed that while her mouth was saying one thing, her hands were telling a different story.

A box of Kleenex sat on the table, and Sherry unconsciously took one after another out of the box and shredded it. Before long the pile resembled a sizable bird's nest.

Finally Daniel remarked, "You keep saying you don't feel guilty about this relationship, but I'm not sure I dare believe it. You know why? Because your hands betray you." He pointed to the nest of shredded Kleenex. "I wonder if your sense of guilt isn't about as high as that pile of Kleenex."

She was speechless.

"You know," he continued, "when Jesus came into Jerusalem and everyone was cheering, the Pharisees said, 'Hey! Make them shut up!' And Jesus said, 'If I make them shut up, the stones will cry out.' Sometimes I talk to people who shut up part of themselves, but their gallstones — or ulcers or blood pressure — cry out. Sherry, I think you are crying out through this pile of Kleenex."

Sherry lowered her head and admitted there were things about herself that she hated. "She never admitted guilt, but she did talk about her loss of self-respect," Daniel recalled. "Her bravado was really a cover-up for her self-hate. We talked honestly, and she and Eddie have begun to make progress on their relationship."

In this case, the key was noticing her unconscious nervousness — the clue that the confrontation was striking close to home — and then moving gently but firmly when the defenses began to come down.

The Internal Work

Those who confront need to be aware of internal dynamics. First, the goal is not an emotional experience but a change of the will. As one church history professor puts it, "Don't look for the highs and lows as much as the longs." That's true of people as well as historical movements. Helping those who don't want help takes a persistence and a perseverance — a *long* perspective, not a high.

Another pastor said, "I have to remind myself that the past is not as important as the future. I'm willing to forget point A, B, and C with a person. Those are in the past and can't be helped. What I'm looking for is point E, F, and G. I want to help individuals with the points they have not reached yet."

A second internal adjustment for confronters is to keep responsibility straight. "I have to remember that I am not ultimately responsible for their behavior — they are," said a minister. "My purpose is to help the individual function on his own, not to obey the decisions I make for him."

Other ministers confess a tendency to play the white knight, riding repeatedly to the rescue. "Every once in a while I find myself wondering what's happened to this couple or that person. I'm tempted to call and say 'What's going on? Do you need more help?' Sometimes they do, but more often it's probably more my need to be the great healer than it is something they need. I have to get unhooked from the need to be needed."

Escalating Steps of Intervention

What can pastors do during the period of resistance, when people refuse to accept input from others? How can the barriers be breached?

It is often safe to assume that the person has a reason for his behavior. Most pastors quietly but persistently seek the source of the hurt.

"I've found that almost any time people claim to be atheists, somewhere in their past they've sought answers from Christians and have been rebuffed," says a pastor in Kansas. "I'll say, 'You've been hurt by the church, haven't you?' And they'll say, 'How did you know?' Almost anyone who is resisting help is harboring a hurt."

The job of the confronter is at least partly to identify with the hurt that's causing a person's behavior. That creates an opening that can be used to great effect. The means can be as simple as an earnest question.

Most ministers try repeated loving probes, often simply by finding time for an unrushed talk and asking, "How are you doing? *Really*, how are things going for you at (pick one) work/home/church? I haven't touched base with you for a while. Give me an update." Perhaps this initiative will have to be taken more than once. Sometimes the response is "None of your business," but normally, if they trust the pastor, people will be honest and afterwards will say "Thanks for asking."

At times, this low-key, oblique approach is sufficient.

Richard Evers never realized what he was walking into when he agreed to see Sharla Holland. Sharla was a thirty-year-old mother of four. Her husband, Toby, two years older, was an airline pilot. Both had been regular church attenders. When Sharla asked to talk with him about "child discipline," Richard set up an appointment.

As Sharla began describing their home life, however, Richard quickly saw that, as is often the case, the problem was not with the children, but with the parents. The home Sharla described contained two separate empires. When Sharla was home alone, one set of standards reigned. When Toby was home, another regime took over.

"We bicker constantly," she said. But the problem of two separate discipline styles wound up being only the surface issue.

One of Sharla's offhand comments set off an alarm in Richard's mind. After complaining of Toby's short fuse with the older kids, she said, "But he spoils Joshua, our youngest. At night, he'll cradle Joshua on his lap and read him a book. They usually both fall asleep in the recliner. I have to wake them both to get them to bed."

"How often does that happen?"

"Oh, almost every night," she said. "He seems to spend more quality time with Joshua than he does with me."

Richard wondered what that did to their sex life, but he decided not to raise the issue just yet. He offered Sharla a book on child discipline and suggested she and Toby both read it and come in together to see him the following week.

He wondered if Toby's lack of interest in intimacy with his wife could mean something more was happening. He decided to raise the issue directly but to be indirect in implicating Toby. Richard asked Toby to meet him for lunch. After some casual conversation, Richard said, "As your pastor, I'd like to know how you're doing as a Christian. You're in a tough job. Pilots are away from home a lot. You're alone. I would imagine temptations can be pretty strong. They would be for me!" He consciously tried to avoid any hint of accusation of infidelity; rather, he tried to suggest that the potential for compromise would be there for anyone, and it was OK to talk about it. "How are you coping with that?"

"The best I can," Toby said, but he didn't look Richard straight in the eye. "You're right, it's not easy. You just have to keep yourself busy — have things to do."

Richard asked how it affected his relationship with Sharla, and Toby was equally noncommittal. The lunch ended on polite but hardly intimate terms.

Two days later, however, Toby showed up at Richard's office.

"You knew, didn't you?" he said.

"About what?" Richard asked.

"That I've been seeing someone," Toby said. "I knew it couldn't be kept secret forever. Did Sharla tell you? I wondered if she was beginning to suspect anything."

"No, Sharla didn't tell me. But you're right, it's hard to keep something like that hidden for long. Want to tell me about it?"

Toby explained that he had been seeing a young woman, another employee of the airline, for almost a year. "I've been trying to live in a dream world," he said. "I guess I knew I couldn't have a wife and a mistress, too. But you don't think about the consequences when you get into these things."

That was the beginning of a long road back for Toby. Eventually, he quit the affair, and he and Sharla were able to repair their relationship. The story might not have ended so happily, however, if Richard had not firmly but tactfully taken the initiative to see Toby. His intentional but oblique confrontation helped save a marriage and heal a home.

Tips for Interveners

Confront with tears. In any confrontation, the tendency is for the person being confronted to say, "You don't understand. You don't know what I've gone through." Graciousness, tenderness, and empathy are important even when you have to be firm.

"I've got to feel their pain, and let them know I feel it," says Joel Eidsness of Trinity Bible Church in Phoenix. "When you say the hard things, say them with tears. I've found that people who enjoy confronting make lousy confronters. A psychologist told me a long time ago, 'When you have to confront, be sure to share how you feel — not just with your words but with your body language, your facial features, your tears. Let them know this isn't easy.' It was good advice. People are much more open if they don't feel you enjoy correcting them."

He finds it takes away the impression that the pastor arrogantly thinks he has all the facts, has interpreted them correctly, and knows exactly what the person needs to do.

Confront with strength, not authority. There's a difference between intervening from a position of strength and a position of authority.

Authority means coming down with an imposed order and saying, "You need to stop this because the board (or the pastor or the Bible or the church constitution or the denomination) disapproves."

Intervening from the position of strength is to point out strongly the natural consequences of the present course. "If this keeps up, here's what's going to happen." And perhaps "Some of those things have happened to me, and they hurt like the blazes. Do you really want to do this?"

When talking with Katie, the woman in chapter 5 who was marrying a second nonbelieving husband, her pastor not only spoke of the biblical prohibitions, but also showed her a *Newsweek* article revealing the unfavorable statistics on second marriages working, especially when the marriage takes place within a year of the divorce.

Very few times will a person turn around by being told he is doing something evil or unacceptable. More often change will happen when a person is confronted with what's in his best interest — "Have you considered this consequence?"

Don't fear their tears. "When I was a younger pastor, I was more lenient with people," says David Seamands. "I didn't like to see anyone cry. Now I'm not as afraid of tears. Sometimes, if a person is reduced to tears, it can be the breakthrough you need. Obviously, you are not simply out to manipulate emotions, but you can be direct with the facts — biblical facts, statistical facts, personal experiences with the consequences of such behavior. You cannot afford to let sentiment prevent you from making the person face reality. If the person cries, that does not mean you've done something wrong. It means you may be getting through."

Encourage them to take even small steps of responsibility. Many pastors don't try to straighten out every area of a person's life at once. "I take my model from Elisha with Naaman (2 Kings 5)," says Mike Tucker of Bethany Community Church in Tempe, Arizona. "After Naaman was healed, he asked for some Israeli soil to take back to his homeland so he could worship God there. Elisha did not correct him with a lecture on God not being tied to geographic locale or holy dirt. Naaman wasn't ready for that. His desire to worship God was enough for now. Elisha simply said, 'Go in peace.'

"Another example is Christ. Several times he says, in effect, 'I've got a lot of things to tell you, but I can't tell you yet. You're not ready.' As a pastor, many times I must be sensitive to how much a person can receive. So many times I encourage a small step rather than a total transformation."

One pastor said his approach is to tell counselees not to set up the next appointment on their way out of the office. He specifically tells them, "Call tomorrow to set up an appointment." This is to insure that people have to take some initiative, to invest some effort, so they will take the session more seriously. A small but significant step toward responsibility.

Another pastor was counseling a divorcée who was sleeping with a man five nights a week. "Interestingly, she told me she wouldn't marry the man because he was not a Christian and was not interested in becoming a Christian," said the pastor. "But she had this great need for affection, and no Christian men were interested in her."

Since her previous attempts to cut off the relationship entirely had failed (largely because she didn't really want them to succeed), the pastor decided to aim for a more modest goal.

"I asked if she thought she could cut down to sleeping with him only one night a week. I figured you have to start somewhere, and she wasn't ready to stop seeing him completely. She agreed to try to reduce their contact."

The affair gradually withered. "Today she is walking with God and doing pretty well," the pastor reports. "In fact, she remarried her former husband. The strategy worked that time. I don't usually do it that way. I may never do it that way again. But it has worked."

A counselor in Dallas, Creath Davis, says if he can get a person to agree to break off an affair for six weeks — which doesn't seem totally impossible to most people — he's found that in most cases the feelings fade, and the affair can be ended. "But the agreement must be *no* contact. Not just sexual contact, but no visits, no phone calls, no notes," he says. "Why? Because affairs are not just sexual in their orientation. They usually end up there, but it's the emotional addiction that's tougher to break. But if the lovers can stay apart for six weeks, that's usually enough to help end the addiction."

When small steps are successfully taken, they can be the basis for subsequent major changes. Counselor Robert Carlson writes of two cases where small steps led to life-changing results:

"Lyle and Betty had been struggling. One problem was that Lyle had been raised with four sisters, and he had never learned to take any household responsibilities. Lyle had an affair, and he and Betty separated and finally divorced. After two years, Lyle came to visit his children, who were living with Betty. The conversation was polite and guarded. Betty was cautious, but inside she was praying for a miracle. As the family spent the evening together, Betty noticed how delighted the children were to see their father, and how much like old times it was, but she noticed one other important difference: he carried his own dishes to the kitchen, and he emptied his own ashtrays.

"Eventually they decided to try again and were remarried.

"Seeing even small changes enables people to see the potential of negotiations made in good faith. This provides the loamy soil in which hope grows.

"With Ted and Andrea, the problem was communication. He was in sales, she in education. She would talk about her day at school, and he would respond with advice. She thought *What does he know about it?* She wasn't after answers, only understanding. She grew more and more silent at home. He would try to dig and probe, but of course, you can never make someone else talk.

"We examined the habits and patterns of their interaction. He agreed to 'invite' her to talk about school. She agreed to try to share something. He agreed to *listen* and withhold advice. It was tough at first. He felt obliged to 'help her out.' But gradually he began to change. Then she had the courage to deal with the bigger things in their life."[1]

Make use of other relationships the person holds dear. Pastors have found the people with the most potential for making changes in another person's life are the individuals that person respects most. Sometimes pastors can make use of these already-established relationships.

In his autobiography, Norman Vincent Peale recalls one time he was faced with an emotionally volatile situation.

A fourteen-year-old boy came one day to my office in Kings Highway Church. Sitting on the edge of the chair, he nervously twisted his cap. He was disturbed about something and that it was a painful matter was very clear. I tried to put him at ease.

"What is your given name?" I asked.

"It's Robert and you know my father. I don't know what to do," he stammered.

"Why don't you talk to your father?"

"I can't; I just can't. That's why I've come to you."

"Well, tell me about it and I will help all I can. And remember that as a pastor you can tell me anything in confidence."

"Reverend Peale, is my father straight? Is he a good man?" He seemed to choke up as he put this question.

"Robert, I am not very well acquainted with your father, but to me he seems a fine man and I've never heard anything bad about him. Why do you ask this question?"

"Well, you see, I love my father very much and I've always looked up to him. I think he is great, the finest man in the world." As he made this statement, tears ran down his face.

"I'm sure he is just that, Robert."

"Oh, I hope so. But the other kids have been whispering things so I can hear them about Dad and some woman. Oh, it can't be true, it just can't," he sobbed.

"Now look here, Robert, you must not let your faith in your father be shaken by some stupid whispers by a bunch of kids. You and I are going to believe in your father. But just to give you peace of mind I'll check up a bit."

Next day I telephoned Robert's father for an appointment. "What is it about?" he asked. I told him I had a matter to take up with him. As I sat across the desk from him, I felt that he was somewhat uneasy. I noted the strong resemblance between father and son. "In the job of being a minister we get all kinds of cases and problems," I explained, "and some of them are quite delicate and personal. But we have to do the best we can with each one. We are in the people-helping business."

"Yeah, I get you," he responded impatiently. "But what has this got to do with me? I don't need any help."

"Maybe not, but your son Robert does."

"Robert," he echoed. "What possible trouble could he have that he wouldn't talk to me about?"

I let the matter hang in the air for a few seconds. "You," I said.

He flushed angrily. "What do you mean by that, Reverend? I don't like what you are saying."

"I don't blame you for that, and you may think it is none of my business. I assure you that what must be said to you is most unpleasant for me. But I have to keep faith with your son who loves, no, idolizes you." Then I told him of my conversation with Robert. "I've gone out on a limb in urging him to have faith in you and not to believe those whispers. But in my opinion you are on the edge of absolutely devastating this boy and ruining your relationship with him. What shall I say to Robert; or how do you want me to handle it with him?"

He sat quite still as though in shock, face white. The silence continued until I became concerned about him. Finally he said, "Let me think. May I see you later?" I left him with his thoughts and his problem, and my heart ached not only for the boy but also for his father.

That night, after a meeting at the church I found the boy's father waiting for me outside. We went back and sat in my office.

"I want to level with you, Reverend. I am involved with a woman. I'm a dirty, low-down no-good. My wife is the finest woman in the world. I've done this because I'm dirty in my mind, in my thoughts. I see clearly what I'm doing and it just isn't worth it. I'm a damned fool. But how can I get out of it?"

"Just tell her you're through. And then be through." He didn't say anything, so I continued. "But that is only the start. You not only must get out of it but, more importantly, you have to get it out of you. It is just plain old sin that got you into this mess. And now we need to get sin out of your mind, out of your heart. That is done by your becoming a new person through faith in Christ. Do you want this change to happen in you?"

Suddenly all the pretense dropped from him. "Oh, my God, Reverend, I can't live unless you get me out of this and get me changed. I've got to control my evil thoughts. Lust, that's what it is. It's the evil in me. I'm no good."

This was healthy, the way he was talking, for it was conviction of sins. He made no excuses. He was honest about what he was and what he had done. And that was basic to becoming what he could be. He was also taking another important step: confession. He emptied out all his sneaking and lying and dishonesty and infidelity. He portrayed graphically his inner warfare between good and evil. He saw what he was and the sight was decidedly unpleasant.

Then, it was important to have him see what he could be. "Telephone the woman now and break it up."

"You mean right now, here with you?"

I shoved the telephone over to him. "Tell her you are with your pastor, in confession, and you are changing your life, beginning now."

Red of face, with a shaking hand holding the receiver, he told her exactly that. Slowly he replaced the receiver. "Know what she said?"

"What?"

" 'You're a good man. Better be that.' "

"She is right," I commented. ". . . Now ask the Lord Jesus Christ to forgive and cleanse you from all sin. Tell Him that you believe in Him with all your heart and accept Him now as your Savior."

He did this with deep sincerity and with tears. I repeated that great old verse: "Though your sins be as scarlet, they shall be as white as snow," and the glorious words of Jesus to the woman taken in adultery: "Go, and sin no more."

When he arose from prayer, on his face there was an unforgettable smile mixed with tears, like sunshine after rain. He grasped my hand with a grip like steel. "How can I ever thank you?" he asked.

"Just by keeping the faith with the Lord and being a wonderful father to that terrific boy of yours. And," I added, "by being true . . ."

Some weeks later father, mother, and son stood at the altar of the church as I received them into membership in Christ's Holy Church, into the society of the redeemed. But it was the look on the boy's face that got me. The whispers ceased and the father kept the faith to the end, so powerful was the change that Christ made in him.[2]

These happy endings don't happen every time, perhaps not even a majority of the time, but they occur frequently enough to encourage pastors not to give up hope. And hope is warranted even in what is perhaps the most vexing pastoral situation: working with withdrawn, unwilling family members.

---

1. Robert J. Carlson. "Hope for Hurting Marriages." *Leadership*, vol. 7, no. 1 (Winter 1986), pp. 36–37.
2. Norman Vincent Peale. *The True Joy of Positive Living*. (New York: William Morrow and Co., 1984) pp. 98–101.

NINE

REACHING AN UNWILLING FAMILY MEMBER

I have on my table a violin string. It is free. I twist one end of it and it responds. It is free. But it is not free to do what a violin string is supposed to do — to produce music. So I take it, fix it in my violin and tighten it until it is taut. Only then is it free to be a violin string.

SIR RABINDRANATH TAGORE

I'm a Christian. My husband is not, and he's making life miserable for me. He doesn't want to make our marriage any better. Would you change him?"

It's one of the most frequent, and most difficult, situations for a pastor — dealing with the unwilling family member. At times, this truly is the situation — the husband is simply unwilling to expend any energy to love his wife.

Other times, however, it's hard to get the actual facts of the case. Maybe the husband's unwillingness is only part of the problem. Perhaps the wife needs to make changes that will create the change in her husband.

"It happens all the time," says one pastor in the Northwest. "Our staff jokes about it. If someone tells us 'Everybody else is going crazy!' that's the person who's *driving* everyone crazy. Despite the fact that he or she is the one coming to the pastor, often the person presenting the problem doesn't want help. That person just wants us to 'fix' everyone else."

Josh and Shirley, a couple in that church, are an example. Josh had been involved with several women before he and Shirley both became Christians. After indicating he wanted to grow in Christ, Josh then had another affair, and Shirley kicked him out of the house. He asked for her forgiveness, and she took him back.

But now after any squabble, she kicks him out of the house. "It's become almost a reflex," explains the pastor. "They're so locked into roles where Shirley plays the innocent and Josh the bad guy that they both believe it, even though it's a half-truth at best. That's the way they've lived for seventeen years. When he cleans up one area of his life, she begins looking for something else on which to nail him."

Shirley came into the pastor's office one day to say "Josh did it again. He came home late without telling me. When I confronted him, he raised his voice, and I told him if he couldn't control his anger, he could just get out of the house. So he left."

"How would you like me to help?"

"I don't want to lose my marriage, and my children are upset because Josh is gone, but I can't let him keep acting so bad. Should I let him come back?"

The pastor asked if perhaps when she confronted Josh she could take a different approach to help create a calmer atmosphere. "Some people resist any hint of self-righteousness," he said carefully. "There are two kinds of sins: outward and inward. Josh's may be the visible sins, but we have to make sure no inward attitudes on our part drive him further off."

Immediately he sensed Shirley shut him off.

"He doesn't understand spiritual things, Pastor. Unless I spell things out directly, he doesn't hear." The rest of the conversation went nowhere. She stopped coming to see the pastor after that.

Helping families is a delicate and explosive undertaking. What are the lessons learned by pastors who have defused these powder kegs? How do you apply a deft hand without getting it blown off?

Work with the Willing

Traditional wisdom suggests that working with only one partner in a marriage relationship is not normally successful.

And yet there are success stories. Occasionally the willing partner can learn some new patterns that begin to improve the behavior of the other.

Lutheran pastor and counselor William Backus writes, "I always stipulate at the outset that our target for change will be the behavior of the patient. I deliberately avoid shooting for major changes in the behavior of someone who is not present. . . . The patient and I agree to consider our work successful if he changes in ways which satisfy him. We will never gauge improvement on the basis of whether or not the absent partner changes, but only on positive improvement in the patient. But experience has proven otherwise. In spite of this careful focus on the patient, reports of change in the absent partner keep coming in. . . . Not only does my patient report that he is doing better and feeling better, but also that the behavior of the *other* person in the troubled relationship has improved."

Reports come back: "He's noticed the change in the way I behave, and he likes it. He doesn't stay in his silent moods for days at a time anymore. And it's been weeks since he lost his temper and swore at me."[1]

What are some of the changes in the willing spouse that can affect the unwilling partner?

1. *A new courage.* One frequent difficulty in marriage is when one partner begins finding his or her greatest satisfaction outside that relationship. Perhaps it's a preoccupation with tennis or fishing or a career or aerobics or another person. In many cases, strangely, the neglected partner never raises the issue.

"My husband is never home," Eloise told her pastor. "He cares more about the job than about me. He'd rather work than see our kids' soccer games."

"Have you told him you feel this way?"

"Oh, no. He'd never listen. Besides he ought to see this himself."

The pastor encountered surprising resistance to the idea of raising the subject with her husband. She seemed to think he would turn into a boogieman. So the pastor tried to get her to think the unthinkable. Boogies tend to shrink when exposed to light.

"What's the worst that would happen if you did tell him how you feel?"

"Oh, it would be terrible."

"How terrible? If you said, 'John, I'm concerned that you're working so many evenings the kids are feeling neglected,' what specifically would he do?"

"He probably wouldn't pay attention."

"Is that so bad?"

"He might blow up."

"How badly would he react? Would he murder you?"

"Well, no."

"Do you think he would hit you?" the pastor asked, recognizing that if the answer were yes, then he'd touched one of the real issues.

But in this case, Eloise said, "Oh, no. He wouldn't do that."

"Would he raise his voice? Would he turn and walk out?"

"Yes, he'd probably yell. He'd say I don't appreciate him."

"Is that so awful?" Eloise seemed surprised that her pastor thought it would be OK to have her husband shout at her.

"But I can't stand raised voices."

"I'm not so sure about that. I think you could tell your husband that you appreciate him so much that you'd like to have him around a few evenings each week," said the pastor. "Even if he yells, I think that would be a good investment in the health of the marriage. Could you picture his anger as a mosquito bite rather than a sword thrust?"

Eloise never did say anything to her husband, but over the next few weeks, as the counseling continued, she reported her husband was staying home more and the home atmosphere was less tense. She thought the change came out of the blue, but the pastor says, "I think it was a result of Eloise broadcasting different vibes, even though they were unconscious. She realized she could have some expectations for her husband, and that unspoken message began coming across."

Even small changes in the one partner can yield enormous

effects on the other. Another woman came to her pastor rather embarrassed.

"My husband reads pornographic magazines, watches X-rated videos, adult cable TV, and all that stuff. Then he wants me to go around the house bare-breasted. Once he had some buddies over for movies, and he insisted I serve refreshments braless. What should I do?"

Since both the husband and the wife were members of the church, the pastor said, "I want to talk with your husband, but I want to talk to you first. If your husband wants you bare-breasted and braless privately for him, that's one thing. Don't fight him, but tell him you draw the line at making yourself available for voyeurs. Tell him you won't stand for it because you have children and because you have dignity."

After a couple days to give the wife a chance to discuss it with her husband, the pastor called the husband and asked him to stop by the church for a visit. The next day, after work, the husband dropped by.

"I talked with your wife this week, and she indicated she was uncomfortable with some of your sex-oriented practices at home. She mentioned specifically that you wanted her braless when you had some friends over. Is that true?"

"Yeah," he said, slouching in the chair.

"She said she felt like she was on display. Did you know she was uncomfortable?"

"Aw, she made too much out of that. I was just having fun. She should be flattered I still think she has a great body."

"Do you think a Christian should be demanding those things of his wife? Do you think it's healthy to be reading off-color literature or looking at those kinds of films?"

"I enjoy them."

"They may be enjoyable to you, but that sounds pretty selfish, don't you think? You're responsible for your wife and children, too. Would you want your daughter, at sixteen, to go baring her breasts for a stag party?"

"Well, no."

"That's what you're asking of your wife. Sex is meant to be

enjoyed but not exploited." He and the husband eventually agreed that sexuality should be a private relationship between a man and his wife only.

A month later, the pastor called the wife. "How are things going?"

"He still watches things I don't care for, but he's doing much better."

"Has all this ruined your sexuality in marriage?"

"Not at all," she replied. "I appreciate it more when I have some dignity."

2. *A renewed power to love.* At times, when dealing with only half the marriage relationship, the love has to be unilateral for a while. At these times, it's especially important to pray for the power to love. Not much affection may be coming from the other spouse, but gradually, the ice may thaw.

One woman told her pastor that her husband wanted a divorce. After discussing the specifics, the pastor said, "Let's do something drastic. Could you try loving him so much that you refuse to get upset even when he *wants* you to get upset?" She agreed to give it a try, and they prayed for God to give her the strength to be loving even when love was resisted.

That night when her husband came home, she asked, "Honey, what would you like for dinner?"

"I don't want to eat with you," he snapped. He walked past her, turned on the TV, and sat there until midnight.

She called her pastor the next day, and again they prayed that God would give her the power to love. That night when her husband came home, she again asked, "What would you like me to fix you, dear?"

"Spaghetti," he said. "But I don't want to eat with you." She ignored the put-down, served him the spaghetti in front of the TV, and let him eat by himself.

For two weeks, he continued to tell her he didn't want her around. She held her emotions in check, releasing them only to God in times of prayer with her pastor.

"The third week, the husband finally broke down," reports the pastor. "He admitted to his wife that he'd been acting worse than a child. He started crying, and they both came in for counseling at that point."

Thanks to God's power, one person made a huge difference in the whole relationship.

3. *An ability to turn criticism into contact.* Love does not always mean passively receiving the criticism and nonverbal insults of another. At times criticism can be turned into a relationship-building experience.

A minister in Massachusetts began giving one woman some suggestions of ways she could respond differently to her husband's verbal abuse. "Instead of just clamming up and listening to his diatribes," he said, "try to enter in firmly but compassionately. You can retain your self-respect without becoming your husband's adversary."

"How?"

"Let's role play a situation. You act the part of your husband," said the minister. "I'll show how you can respond."

The woman played the part passionately, complaining about pressures at work and how miserable it is to come home to a wife who doesn't meet his needs.

"In other words, you feel absolutely drained of any enthusiasm for your work," the counselor-turned-wife said, restating the charge. "Am I reading you right?"

"Yes, absolutely."

"And you feel like I have been largely responsible for the draining. Is that what you're saying?"

"I sure am."

"Boy, that really hurts me to hear that. I hate to think I'm doing that to you. Is there anything else I've done to hurt you?"

"Now that you mention it, I can't stand it to come home and see you watching TV. Is the news more important than I am?"

"You feel I ignore you when you come home?"

"That's right."

"I'm sorry. Maybe I've been missing some things. I do need help to see things through your eyes. What can I do to help the situation?"

The woman was at a loss. She didn't know what her husband would say.

"Your husband may not know what to say either," said the minister. "But let's find out."

They worked out a five-step process for her to follow when her husband criticized:

- Take him seriously and listen to the criticism.
- Say it back to him to make sure you've heard it correctly.
- Ask if there are any other complaints.
- Restate any additional criticisms.
- Then honestly ask him to help you improve the situation.

When the woman came back two weeks later, she said, "It's totally different now. I'm not just being dumped on; I feel like I've taken more control of the situation. When he criticizes it's because I'm asking him, and it changes the atmosphere because we're looking for solutions instead of just wallowing in complaints."

This exercise turned criticism into contact. It requires a different set of mental muscles to look for constructive ways to redeem the situation than it does to lazily recite complaints. That exercise is good for the husband, good for the wife, good for the marriage.

4. *A deeper understanding of the factors.* Active listening also leads to seeing things from the other person's point of view — almost always a helpful exercise.

One woman had tried for years to get her domineering husband to come to the pastor for marriage counseling. He refused. Finally, something within her seemed to snap. The children were raised; she decided to leave him. She got a job and made plans to move out. Suddenly *he* was the one wanting them both to see the pastor. He was ready to own up to his failings in the past, but she was saying, "I really like this new life. He wasn't attentive to my needs for twenty-five years. Now I'll make up for it." She seemed ready to leave both family and spiritual roots behind.

Her husband finally got her to agree to see the pastor before she made any final decision.

"We talked about the aggravations she felt regarding her

husband," said the pastor. "I asked such questions as *Why do you think he's like that? What caused him to be insensitive?* Especially as I met with her alone, I tried to help her see his inability to meet her needs not as an offense but as a handicap — coming out of weakness and fear. I tried to paint a picture of him as relationally wounded, limping. He wasn't consciously trying to demean her. She began to feel compassion toward him instead of resentment. To me it was a case of 'perfect love casting out fear' — and resentment."

She decided to try to salvage their marriage. They wound up staying together.

Helping people reframe their image of the situation from being victims of a conscious attack to being involved with a person who has deep wounds can encourage compassion and cast out fear, guilt, anxiety, resentment, and a whole host of negative feelings.

Another counselor said she's found a helpful image.

"I was in a fire and badly burned a few years ago," she said. "Even now, I can't sit across the room from a fireplace. My skin is still too sensitive to heat. I use that story with people who are 'burn victims' themselves, or perhaps living with someone who was 'burned.' I explain that some people were abused as children — or maybe were torn down in some way. This burn leaves them oversensitive to certain things. Now whenever a spouse raises a voice even a little bit for emphasis, they recoil because the 'burn' is still sensitive."

The key, she says, is to help the willing partners begin to look for ways they, or their unwilling spouses, have been singed in the past. That, too, builds compassion and understanding.

Involve the Unwilling Spouse

At times, however, working only with the willing spouse isn't enough. Some contact needs to be made with the unwilling partner if the problem is to be solved. How can that be done most effectively?

One way is taking the initiative to track down the person.

For this to work, however, the first step is getting permission from the willing spouse to use his or her name. And at times, that takes some coaxing.

The "you need to confront my husband, but you can't let him know I've been talking to you" setup is virtually impossible to handle. It creates an unnatural situation. The person being confronted will inevitably ask, "How did you find out about me?" and you can't say you read it in a fortune cookie.

A Methodist pastor has three questions he poses to anyone who wants him to confront someone else:

— Have you already tried confronting him yourself?

— Would you be willing to sit with me as I talk with him?

— Will you allow me to say you suggested I talk with him?

"If the answer to all three questions is no, then it's obvious they care more for their reputation than for solving the problem. And I'm not going to intervene. I've got to be able to indicate what I know and who told me."

Other pastors have found it relatively nonthreatening to ask the unwilling spouse to come "as a resource person."

One woman was having problems with her husband, who had nothing to do with the church and wanted nothing to do with counseling. The pastor recognized a need to talk with him, but how?

"I called him and said, 'I've been talking with your wife for the last several weeks. She's got some real struggles in terms of who she is as a person and the relationship the two of you have. I'm not here to lay blame on either of you, but I want to help her the best I can, and I need your objective point of view. Would you be willing to come in and let me bounce some things off you? I need some feedback on how I might best help her.' It's amazing how many men come! They assume you have a professional interest and professional skills, and often they're willing to help solve 'their wife's' problem."

When the husband, in this case, does come, the approach is important. Integrity demands you do precisely what you told him when you invited him to come.

"The first thing I do is try and put him at ease," the pastor continued. "I repeat that I'm not here to knock him over the head but that I want to share a couple of the things Mary Jane has told me. This is the way she perceives what is going on in the relationship, and I wanted to see if her observations were accurate or not. Then I mention a couple of things and say, 'Can you help me with that? This is the way she perceives it. How do you perceive it? And what do you sense is going on in the relationship?' "

This helps form a therapeutic alliance with the husband, and often he quits seeing the pastor as a prosecutor coming to indict him and instead begins to see him as a friend who can help ease a painful part of life.

The next step, after the unwilling spouse indicates willingness to enter into joint counseling as a participant rather than a colleague, is to identify with the hurts the unwilling spouse feels. In most cases he is sure the pastor is going to be on the wife's side because she has already talked to the pastor about him. He resists counseling because he's sure it's going to be two against one.

One pastor, who does lots of family counseling, has found one way to break through that barrier. "I often begin by saying, 'There is a reason why you feel so much pain and why you have experienced this pain for all these years. You've probably come now to the point of hopelessness and despair, so much so that you don't even want to talk about it. When I see people in that much pain, I hurt with them.' In other words, I try to side with this person, recognizing the real pain, and saying 'I want to be a friend as you go through this time in your life. I know it hurts to even think of talking about it. And it's been this way so long, it seems hopeless that any solution would ever be possible.'

"I make that speech when I first begin counseling; I even make that speech from the pulpit! When people begin to see that you mean it, it really opens the door. But that message has to be communicated over and over. Once isn't enough. People have to see it is a consistent attitude."

While not a guaranteed means to reaching unwilling

spouses, these approaches do increase the odds of enlisting their help.

Beware the "Obvious Culprit"

In many family counseling situations, pastors find the obvious culprit is often not the real culprit.

"When a wife runs off in an affair, quite often we think, *She's obviously doing wrong,* turn away from her, and focus our love and support on the husband," observes a pastor from Southern California. "The wounded man does need our love and care, but it's a mistake to withdraw from the person we've labeled the sinner. The question we need to ask is *Why did she do that? What was wrong in the marriage?* When you start digging, you may find the husband was more at fault ultimately than the wife."

One of the other family situations where the obvious culprit is often not the real culprit involves the rebellious child.

Granted, even the best parents have children who choose wrong directions. But the frequent lament of pastors is that whenever you hear a parent saying "Straighten out my kid," you can almost start looking for the problem between husband and wife that has prompted the child's behavior. When pastors begin working with the teen who "doesn't want help," they discover in many cases the parents are the ones who don't realize their need to become better parents.

Warren and Gloria Evans came to see Pastor Todd Frederick because they were worried about Andrew, their seventeen-year-old. The Evanses were solid church members, and Andrew usually attended youth group functions, although he seemed to remain on the fringe.

"He's a liar and a thief," said Warren, after sitting down in Todd's office. "He constantly steals from his brother and sister. He even steals from his friends at school, and you can't believe a thing he says."

"What does he lie about?" Todd asked.

"That's what's strange. He lies about things that don't even matter," said Gloria. "He lies even when the truth would be to his benefit. For instance, he told us he'd gone to a movie with a friend from school whom we don't particularly like. Later we found out he'd gone skating with the church youth group. Or we'll be discussing a particular TV show at the dinner table, and he'll say, 'I didn't see it,' and later we'll find out he did. It doesn't make any difference if he did or didn't. But why the lie?"

"That's not as bad as his stealing," inserted Warren. "He's stolen money from my wallet. He goes over to a friend's house and steals a ring from his friend's dresser. What's the problem with him?"

Todd admitted he didn't know, but he said he'd like to talk with Andrew.

It took a couple sessions before Todd could get anything more than grunts, downcast eyes, and a mumbled "I don't know" from Andrew. But when he did begin to open up, Andrew painted a different family picture than Todd had previously seen. Andrew's complaint was that his mom and dad gave preferential treatment to Julie, his sixteen-year-old sister.

"She's Miss Good Little Christian," said Andrew. "I feel left out of the family. She gets all the special privileges, and I get none."

Todd raised the obvious point. "Well, Julie doesn't behave as badly as you do. Your parents don't give you permission to do things because you haven't been trustworthy. Aren't you always grounded because of something you've done?"

Andrew turned the charge around. "No," he said, suddenly animated. "I disobey because they make rules that I have to obey and she doesn't."

At first, Todd assumed it was natural sibling rivalry. But as he got specifics from Andrew, there truly was a preference shown.

"Dad likes to hunt, and I hate it," said Andrew. "But in order to spend 'quality time with his son,' he drags me off hunting. I'd rather do anything else, but that's the only time we spend together. When he spends time with Julie, *she* gets to pick the time and place."

He continued with increasing energy. "If I want money, I have to earn it. But they give her an allowance. It's not fair. She can drive the car and doesn't have to put gas in it, but when I bring it home, it better be filled up! When I come home, Mom and Dad don't even say hi before they ask 'What have you been up to? Where have you been?' I feel like a criminal even when I haven't done anything."

Todd had to admit there was more here than simple age difference between Andrew and Julie. But he could also understand why Warren and Gloria showed preference to Julie — she was the good kid. She could be trusted. Andrew was harder to like and harder to trust. But Todd decided to ask Warren and Gloria about it.

He knew he needed to broach the subject delicately. So he asked just the two of them to stop by the church. He began, "It's taken some time, but I've finally gotten Andrew to open up a little bit. We may not agree with his opinions, but I think it's important at least to respect what he's saying. Andrew says he feels there are some major differences in the way you deal with him compared with how you deal with Julie. He thinks you have different attitudes toward the two of them. Do you think there could be anything to that?"

"Good grief," said Warren. "We love our children equally, but of course we're happier with Julie's behavior than Andrew's. Hers is acceptable; Andrew's is not."

"Let me mention a couple of specifics Andrew raised," Todd said gently, and he relayed Andrew's observations about the hunting trips, the allowance, and the gas policy for the family car. "Those are some examples of what Andrew feels is unfair. Right now, though, I'm not as concerned about Andrew's opinion as yours. You're closer to the situation than I am. Do you think those things are fair?"

As they discussed them one by one, Warren and Gloria admitted they'd never considered the possibility that Andrew felt wronged, but they didn't think what they were doing was unjustified. "Maybe he does have a point," Gloria said. "If you see it through the eyes of a teen, it would make you angry."

"But we still can't tolerate lies and stealing!" Warren said.

"No, and we won't," said Todd. "Let me work with him on that. But in the meantime, let me give you a homework assignment: Simply observe one another. Warren, I want you to see how Gloria deals with Andrew and Julie. Just stand back and watch her. And Gloria, I want you to see how Warren deals with the kids for the next two weeks. Try to be objective. Ask yourselves *Is what I'm doing fair?* And a second thing. I'll be working with Andrew on his lying. If he admits to telling a lie, I don't want you to jump on him or demand to know why he lied. Just calmly tell him thanks for telling the truth this time."

Warren and Gloria accepted the assignment for the next two weeks.

When Todd met with Andrew that week, he told him what he'd discussed with his parents, then he said, "But one way you can begin to show yourself worthy of their trust is to stop stealing and lying."

"I don't know if I can stop lying," said Andrew. "Sometimes I have to."

"I won't argue with that," said Todd. "But do you think you could lie less frequently?"

"Probably."

"Would you be willing to quit lying about little things? I mean, if it doesn't matter if you went to 7-Eleven or to McDonald's, tell your parents the truth."

"Sometimes I lie before I even think about it," Andrew said.

"At some point in your mental process you must think to yourself *Well, I actually went to McDonald's, not 7-Eleven.*"

"But then I don't want to tell them I lied."

"Let me give you an assignment, Andrew. I want you to tell your parents when you lie. I've told them not to get on your case. I just want you to stop and say 'No, no. I'm sorry. I didn't go to 7-Eleven. I went to McDonald's.' Can you do that?"

"I'll try."

"That's all I ask."

Two weeks later, Warren and Gloria returned and admitted that some of Andrew's observations were valid. "Maybe we have been somewhat uneven in our treatment of Andrew and Julie," said Gloria. "Andrew does have a right to be angry and to want more attention than he's been getting."

"We just naturally thought Andrew was the one with the problem," said Warren. "It never occurred to us that our handling of things contributed."

At that point, Todd began meeting with the whole family and talking through their expectations and policies.

"It helped a great deal," says Todd. "Andrew's lying has gradually stopped, even about big things. He stopped getting in trouble in school. Things are going pretty well now."

The key was recognizing where the real problem lay. It was not Andrew's rebellion. It was the *cause* of Andrew's rebellion. When the investigation went back far enough in the cause/effect relationships, it was able to avoid the temptation to settle for the obvious culprit and miss the real issue.

Another pastor observes, "We're finding more and more that we need to get the whole family involved in counseling. For us to deal just with the one who's knocked on the office door, or just the one who's being pointed at, is not usually helpful at all."

Relational problems involve more than one person. It isn't that "my kid has a problem" or "my spouse has a problem." No, *we* have a problem. It's hard to rebel in isolation. Helping those who don't want help means involving the whole network.

---

1. William Backus. *Telling Each Other the Truth*. (Minneapolis: Bethany House, 1985) pp. 17–18.

TEN

A FAMILY THAT RISKED THE RELATIONSHIP

It is since Christians have largely ceased to think of the other world that they have become so ineffective in this. Aim at heaven and you will get earth thrown in; aim at earth and you will get neither.

C. S. LEWIS

O ne of the ways to begin help-
ing people who don't want help, as we've already seen, is
developing a relationship they value. At times, however, that
very relationship must be risked. Perhaps no place is this
more painful than within the pastor's own family.

No matter how solid their relationship with their children,
most parents still feel a tremor of anxiety as a son or daughter
leaves the nest. What kinds of choices will he or she make?
What if those choices are foolish or self-destructive? What if
the young people need help to avoid a terrible mistake but
don't want help — or don't have the strength to accept it? The
years after high school can be a time of awkward transition —
a twilight world between accountability and independence.

What follows is the story of one family that agonized over
that tension. Not all pastoral families would choose to handle
this situation the same way. But this family's story holds some
vital clues for others in similar situations.

Bill and Maryann Harris had worked hard over the years to
show their children that being raised in a pastor's home not
only meant certain responsibilities, like being a perennial

example in the youth ministry, but also afforded some privileges, like enjoying a privileged relationship with the church's guest speakers and visiting missionaries.

Their two oldest children apparently enjoyed life in the parsonage. After going to college on a football scholarship, Martin went to seminary and became a church planter, and Brenda attended a Christian college and joined the staff of an inner-city youth ministry. While both were confident, capable workers, neither was quite as strong-willed as the youngest, Caryl.

Through her high school years, Bill and Maryann considered Caryl's self-confidence one of her greatest virtues. Her standards were high. She didn't want to limit herself to dating one guy. "I don't want to be seen as anyone's 'property,' " she would say. She enjoyed going out with a guy from church one night and a guy from school the next night — "double dating," she called it.

Maryann and Caryl often talked about the guys Caryl was seeing. "Some of the girls at school have to sneak out to see their boyfriends," Caryl said. "I wouldn't want to date anyone I wasn't proud to bring home to meet my folks."

After high school, since Caryl enjoyed making her own clothes, she decided to attend a school that offered courses in fashion design. She enrolled at a State university two hours from home. It was far enough to afford some independence but close enough to allow visits home once a month. In addition, during her first year, Caryl would call home every week with another story about dorm life. She especially enjoyed telling about her attempts to be a Christian in a secular setting.

One night she reported the following conversation with two of the guys on her floor, Mitch and Tony, who had come to her room.

"Is it true what we hear — that you don't drink alcohol?" they asked.

"It is," said Caryl.

"You mean you've never had a beer or a glass of wine?"

"I don't even drink Nyquil!" Caryl laughed.

"I can't believe it!" Tony said.

"I've never met anyone who hasn't had a drink," said Mitch. "We'll have to change that!"

"Why?" Caryl countered. "You have all kinds of friends who drink. Wouldn't you like to have one friend who doesn't? After all, wouldn't it be nice to have someone who can drive straight after a party?"

Before they went back to their own room, the guys had admitted she had a point.

Bill and Maryann enjoyed the story. They encouraged Caryl to keep trying to fit in without violating her standards.

"A campus is a tough place to be 'in the world but not of the world,' " Bill told Maryann after putting the phone down. "But it sounds like Caryl's doing a pretty good job."

Caryl met with some Christians in her dorm once a week for breakfast, Bible study, and prayer. She also attended a Tuesday night Bible study for college students at the Baptist church near the campus.

Bill and Maryann suspected nothing unusual, then, when Caryl called one week during her sophomore year to say that "a couple of guys in the dorm are in love with me."

"They've already sent me a dozen roses and a box of chocolates," she said with her characteristic laugh. "I marched down the hall and gave them back the chocolates. I told them my figure couldn't handle the calories, but I did appreciate the flowers — they weren't fattening."

"Which guys were they?" Maryann asked.

"Mitch and Tony."

"Isn't that an unusual gift for them to give you?"

"Oh, I don't know," said Caryl. "We've got a pretty close group here on the floor. It's sort of nice; it's been a while since any guys have shown a special interest in me. Maybe I've been spending too much time in the library." She laughed. "Don't worry, Mom. They're harmless."

Over the next few weeks, Bill and Maryann kept hearing more and more about Tony and Mitch, especially Mitch. Caryl reported on conversations they had at supper. She mentioned that Mitch offered to walk her home from Tuesday night Bible study.

"Mitch is in the Bible study, too?" Maryann asked.

"No, I invited him, but he says he's not the 'religious' type," Caryl replied. "He just doesn't think I should be walking across campus alone at night. Besides, he's usually coming back from the library, so it's not out of his way. I appreciate the company."

Whenever Caryl went to football games or out for pizza, Bill and Maryann noticed, Mitch's name was usually mentioned as part of the group.

During Christmas break while Caryl was home, the university's basketball team was playing a local college. Mitch was in town to see the game and invited Caryl to go with him. "I'm not all that keen on going with Mitch," she told her mom, "but since I've met some of the basketball players at school, I do enjoy seeing them play."

When Mitch came to pick her up, Bill and Maryann met him for the first time. Bill's first impression was that Mitch's West Texas accent made him sound almost a hayseed. His boots and Stetson added to the image. Mitch was a pre-veterinary student, and he seemed friendly enough, asking, "Should I get Caryl back any time in particular?"

"I appreciate you asking," said Bill. "Just keep it reasonable."

After Mitch and Caryl had left for the game, Bill told Maryann, "He seems like a nice guy, but hardly Caryl's type. They're from totally different backgrounds. She says he gets good grades, but you'd never know it by listening to him."

That night after Mitch brought her home, Caryl told Maryann, "We had a good time. Mitch really knows basketball, and he explains the strategy real well. And afterward, since Mitch knows all the players, we went out to eat with them. I felt like an 'insider.' I do wish he hadn't ordered his beer; I don't usually go out with guys who drink, but he's a sharp guy and maybe I can be a good influence on him. He could use a Christian friend. He said one of the reasons he likes me is because I have strong moral standards."

In the weeks that followed, the Harrises heard more and more about Mitch — about the new Ford pickup he drove, about his dreams of establishing his own veterinary hospital, about the times he took Caryl to cattle and horse shows. "I only wish he'd clean up his language," said Caryl.

Bill and Maryann didn't say much about the budding friendship until one day Caryl mentioned that Mitch teased her a lot about going to the Bible study. He called Christians "the Great Pretenders," suggesting they live in a make-believe world. Caryl said, "I told him that wasn't true, that *I* was a Christian who tried to keep her feet on the ground." Mitch's response was "Well, you're OK, but all the guys at that Bible study are flyweights."

"I didn't have an answer for that," Caryl said. "I had to admit none of the guys in the fellowship are real sharp."

"It's too bad he can't meet some of the Christian athletes who've spoken at our church," Maryann said.

"Yeah," said Caryl, somewhat absently.

"He's not out to undermine your faith, is he?" Maryann asked.

"Oh, Mom, don't be paranoid," Caryl said. But for the first time, Maryann felt a flutter in her stomach.

When Caryl told her parents that Mitch continued to try to get her to go drinking with him, Bill and Maryann suggested that maybe Mitch wasn't the friend he seemed to be. "If he knows your standards, why does he keep trying to get you to change them?" Caryl didn't have an answer.

Apparently, she mentioned to Mitch that her parents were not overjoyed with their friendship. The next time she called she managed to work into the conversation that "Mitch was asking me if I felt restricted growing up in a preacher's home, if my parents always chose my friends for me. He told me his parents gave him a free rein." Bill and Maryann chose not to debate the issue, feeling that they didn't need to defend their approach to parenting.

In February, Bill got an invitation to preach at the Baptist church next to the university, and Caryl brought several of her dorm friends, including Mitch, to hear him. Mitch seemed relaxed during the service, but afterward Caryl said, "Mitch was pretty uncomfortable. He had never attended anything but an occasional Mass before, and he didn't even tell his folks he was coming with me today." All of them were encouraged that at least he came. But the experience seemed only to prompt increased antagonism from Mitch.

"I don't see why you go to that church," he told Caryl. "They're so narrow. They take their religion too seriously."

"It *is* important to us," said Caryl. "But that doesn't mean we're fanatics. We enjoy life, too. We just want to enjoy *all* of life, including spiritual life now and eternal life in heaven."

"But it's different from the way I was raised," he said. "We're religious, too, but we party and have a good time. And my parents don't continue to try to control my life."

When they heard about that, Bill and Maryann began to fear that Mitch was not only attacking Caryl's faith, but also trying to sabotage her relationship with them. "But maybe we *are* being paranoid," Maryann said. "She does have to grow up." Bill remained silent.

What they both did notice, however, was that when Caryl called home, she wouldn't mention Mitch unless she was asked, and even then, Bill and Maryann got the impression she didn't want to talk about him — a definite change from a month before.

During spring break, Caryl came home for the week, and Mitch stopped by one night to take her out. When they returned, around 3 A.M., Mitch's loud good-bye — spinning tires and a blast on the horn of his pickup — woke Maryann. She slipped on her robe and went downstairs.

"Sorry about the noise, Mom," Caryl said, laughing nervously. "Mitch is a little rowdy at times."

"How was your evening?"

"We had a good time."

"I'm glad. Where did you go?" Maryann asked, trying not to appear the inquisitor.

"We saw a movie, and then went out to, uh, a place to eat."

"A place I should go sometime?"

"If you must know, Mom, it was The Fiddlestring. It's a country music place that Mitch really likes. He likes to two-step. It's fun."

"I thought you had to be twenty-one to go there."

"You're supposed to be, but they didn't check our I.D.'s"

Maryann decided to wait until morning to say anything more.

At breakfast, Bill and Maryann pointed out that Caryl had changed considerably from the time when she took pride in being the only one in the dorm who didn't drink, to now, when she was defending Mitch for taking her to a bar, even though she was under age.

"I didn't drink. I just went to dance," she said.

"Seems to me it's living a lie just being there," said Bill. "And I don't like you riding with Mitch after he's been drinking. You used to look down on the kids in high school who snuck off to drink and spend time with boyfriends. You've changed."

"I guess that's just the way I am," Caryl said. She refused to admit any wrongdoing or say she wouldn't do it again. Bill and Maryann hoped this was just one of those minor crises of growing up and testing her independence. They wanted to tell Caryl to stop seeing Mitch, but they weren't ready to risk their increasingly strained relationship.

For the rest of the school year, though slightly defensive about Mitch, Caryl still was open about their activities. She mentioned that late one night he knocked on her door, and she could tell he was drunk so she refused to let him in. "He sometimes gets violent and throws things when he's been drinking," she said.

She mentioned that he'd asked her to wash his truck, so she did. She was watching her weight because Mitch had said something about her pants getting tight. And she told how the Bible study group was demanding more time, and she thought she was going to have to drop it from her schedule next year.

Bill and Maryann hoped that the summer break, when Mitch returned to his dad's veterinary clinic and Caryl came home to work, would also mean a breakup in their relationship. But it didn't. They may have been apart, but the weekly letters and phone calls showed the ties were still there.

"Maybe we should accept Mitch as a given and try to work with him," said Maryann.

"Go ahead," said Bill. "But their relationship will never work. They're too different. I just wish Caryl could see that."

That fall, they told Caryl to invite Tony and Mitch home for a Sunday afternoon picnic. When she did, however, Mitch told her, "I don't have to go there. I've already met your folks." Bill wondered what had caused the hostility. After all, they had only met face to face twice — once before Mitch and Caryl's date to the basketball game, and once at Sunday dinner with the group from the dorm after he had preached near the university. Whatever the reason, throughout Caryl's junior year, the hostility between Mitch and the Harrises increased, trapping Caryl in the middle.

At the beginning of the year, Caryl had said, "I'm going to be twenty in October. Let's plan something fun for my birthday." So Maryann began making plans: a party on Saturday night with some of her friends from high school and Sunday dinner with some friends from their church.

On Tuesday, however, Caryl called to say "Mitch wants to take me to Dry Lake this weekend to celebrate my birthday."

"But we've planned a celebration here," Maryann said. "Can't you cancel?"

Maryann took a deep breath and said, "No, we can't."

"Well, Mitch isn't going to like this. He wants me to go home and meet his parents."

"I'm sorry," said Maryann, not used to being this forceful. "Everyone's already invited. I think you should come home."

Caryl finally agreed, but as she predicted, Mitch was furious. "You can't make any decisions yourself," he shouted. "Your parents make them for you. They rule your life. They'll never set you free. You're a slave." Caryl denied it.

Mitch stalked off, swearing. "Forget you, woman. You're hopeless."

When she came home that weekend, Caryl said, "I've done a lot of crying the last couple days. It's over between Mitch and me; I had no business going with him anyway. I actually feel relieved." Maryann felt relieved, too, but Bill suspected the war was not yet over.

For her birthday, Bill and Maryann let Caryl take their second car, an aging Ford Fairmont, back to school. She had a part-time job in a fabric store, and now she wouldn't have to walk or ride buses at night — or get rides from Mitch.

Mitch ignored Caryl for two weeks and then suddenly re-entered the picture, ready to pick up where they'd left off. He asked her to type one of his papers. Caryl said OK. Then she helped him wash his truck. Soon they were dating again, and she was cleaning his room and doing his laundry. She bought cowboy boots and jeans "because Mitch thinks they look good on me" and began wearing red fingernail polish "because Mitch likes it."

"And he accuses us of keeping her a slave," Bill muttered to Maryann after one of the weekly phone calls.

Caryl did put her foot down at times, although feebly. After one party featuring "chugging contests," Caryl told him she didn't feel comfortable around drinking games and would not go to any more of those parties.

"You better learn to like them," he said.

"I don't think I have to," she replied, but as the months went by, she stopped resisting and went wherever he wanted.

At every opportunity, Bill and Maryann were encouraging her to break off the relationship, to spend more time with friends from the Bible study.

"Caryl, we just don't see any future in this," Maryann said. "Mitch is really very, very different, and I don't see any hope that he's going to change. We've prayed for him. And remember when you told him why you were a Christian? You shared your testimony, and he said, 'Don't you ever talk to me like that again. I like the way I live. I'm not going to change.' Until he shows some sign of softening, there's really no solid foundation for a relationship to be built."

Without being absolutely demanding, they tried everything they could: pointing out areas of incompatibility and insensitivity, trying to clarify Mitch's tendency to be critical of the faith, raising questions about the direction things were going.

"Mitch seemed to have more and more power over her, and she wasn't able to break it," reflected Maryann. "She would say, 'Well, there are no Christian guys who are interested in me' or 'There are no Christian guys who have the same charisma he has. He's so masculine; he takes charge.' She complained about Christian guys, but since she'd stopped going to the Bible study and church activities, she wasn't any place where she could meet them. Her life revolved around her small circle of friends in the dorm."

One night, over the phone, Caryl said, "I like Mitch because he has goals. He knows where he's going."

"Assertiveness may be attractive to a certain point," said Bill. "But I think you'll find it can become oppression and control four years into marriage. With him you would be a nonperson."

"All the Christian guys I know are losers," she said. "Non-Christian guys treat me better than the Christian guys I know."

"As a male, it's hard for me to respond," said Bill. "But I do know it's not worth mortgaging your soul for any relationship with a man."

As Bill recalls, at this point things seemed to become less rational. "Caryl's emotional responses didn't seem to have any pattern. One day she seemed to agree that she wanted to live the way she'd been brought up, but then the next day she would be angry at us for raising any question of right or wrong."

Mitch graduated at Christmas of Caryl's junior year and went to Argentina to work with an uncle on a cattle ranch. The Harrises breathed a sigh of relief, thinking perhaps he was gone. He did write Caryl several letters, a few of which she let Maryann read.

"He used so many obscene words I was embarrassed," Maryann told Caryl. "Doesn't he care who he's using that language around?"

"Oh, that's just Mitch," Caryl said.

"How can you stand it?"

Caryl just shrugged.

When Mitch returned to Texas, Caryl was home for spring break. One evening around 5 P.M., he phoned to see if she was free for dinner. She said yes, but Mitch didn't show up until after 10. Caryl met him at the door. Maryann stood in the background.

"Here I am. Let's go eat!" he said to Caryl, without a glance at Maryann.

"You haven't eaten supper yet?" asked Caryl.

"No. I'm famished. Let's go." And he grabbed Caryl's hand and pulled her out the door. Maryann walked to the door and watched the pickup spray gravel as it sped away.

When 2 A.M. came and went, Bill said to Maryann, "I didn't use to worry about Caryl when she stayed out late because she would always tell us what happened when she got back. But I don't trust Mitch. And after Caryl's been with him, she doesn't like to talk about it."

It was after 3 by the time they got back, and Bill was lying in bed unable to sleep. Maryann, also restless, had stayed up to invite Mitch to spend the night on the downstairs couch. Caryl's hair was mussed and her clothes disheveled.

"Late supper," Maryann said in her most matter-of-fact voice.

"Oh, you know," said Caryl. "It took a while to eat and talk and stuff."

"Well, Mitch, it's too late to try to make it all the way to Dry Lake," Maryann said, trying to retain her composure. "I've fixed the couch for you to camp out." Mitch accepted with a simple "Sounds good."

The next morning, Caryl was up early, hair curled and make-up on, and went to McDonald's for breakfast with Mitch. When they came back, Maryann was in the kitchen, but Bill stayed in his study, trying to read. "I don't think I should see Mitch," he had told his wife. "I don't know if I'll be able to control what I would say."

Caryl walked in to where her mother was reading the newspaper.

"Mitch wants me to go to Dry Lake with him," she said.

Maryann gulped. "I don't think it's a good time to ask after last night, but ask your father." Caryl went upstairs.

Bill said, "Absolutely not. Mitch has earned neither our trust nor our respect. I can't give you my permission." Caryl protested but eventually went downstairs to tell Mitch she couldn't go.

"Well I've never been treated like this before!" Mitch fumed. "Your dad won't even talk to me himself. I guess that's what happens in religious circles."

When he left, neither Caryl nor her parents felt like saying anything to each other. But Maryann tried. "It would take a lot, I know, but if Mitch could become a Christian, it would be like the apostle Paul. He'd sure have a lot of energy and drive to give."

"It'll take just as great a miracle, and until it does," Bill said, looking at Caryl, "it can be dangerous for a Christian to be too close to him."

Maryann turned to Bill. "But don't we have to keep befriending him? If we tell him to leave Caryl alone, what will he think of Christians? What if he winds up in hell because we didn't want him around?"

"Your opinion of God is too small," Bill sighed. "If God is sovereign, I doubt if he's going to allow two parents' concern for their daughter's spiritual life to send someone else to hell. God has plenty of ways to reach Mitch — including Caryl's life standing for something else."

For the rest of the school year, Caryl stayed at the university, and the Harrises could only pray she was making wise choices. Mitch was in Dry Lake, but they knew he made periodic visits to see Caryl. Caryl had mentioned that Mitch had a serious side — he was even talking about how many children he'd like to have. Bill and Maryann didn't know what to say.

That summer, Caryl found a job near the university and decided to stay in Austin. She came home on weekends once or twice a month. One day while Bill was in the church office, working on a sermon, he looked up to see Mitch standing in the doorway.

"I thought it was time we talked face to face," said Mitch.

"That sounds like a good idea," Bill replied.

"I want to know why you don't like me," Mitch demanded.

"We don't dislike you, Mitch. But we can't encourage a relationship between you and Caryl when there is no solid foundation for a lasting relationship. We see such fundamental differences in the way you two were raised."

"Like what?"

Bill tried to explain the differences between Mitch's nominal Christian upbringing and Caryl's active evangelical family. He tried to explain conversion, forgiveness, and living a life that honors God. "Being a Christian is a way of life for our family," he concluded.

"Caryl's told me all that," Mitch said. "I come from a strong family, too. We believe in God and go to church once in a while. There's not that much difference in our beliefs."

Not wanting to deny Mitch's religious heritage, Bill said, "I think I mean something different by commitment to God than you do — it's more than church attendance. I just wish I could explain it more clearly. But Mitch, even if it were true that our religious differences were minor, which they aren't, I think the difference in our backgrounds is such that you two could not be permanently happy together. Part of it is the difference between rural and urban expectations. Part of it is Caryl. You have a strongly traditional view of a woman's role in the home. Caryl has been raised to think for herself, but she has not been herself since she's met you. She's taken by your strong personality, but that won't last in a marriage. Eventually she would feel oppressed. The bottom line is that you two don't belong together."

Mitch reiterated his opinion that they were two grown adults, and he was sure they could work out any differences. He rose to leave. "But I do understand a little more of your opinion," said Mitch.

"I hope I've made myself clear," said Bill. "I appreciate you stopping by."

Both Mitch and Bill left thinking they had won a major battle. Bill told Maryann, "I think Mitch may see we've got good reasons to be opposed to their relationship." And Mitch told Caryl, "I think I got your dad straightened out on things."

The next weekend, when Caryl was home, she said to her mother, "I'm glad things went so well between Mitch and Dad. Mitch said Dad is starting to come around."

"That isn't how I read it," said Maryann. "Dad and I are as opposed as ever. We've prayed that this thing would work out, that Mitch would change. But the only person we've seen change, Caryl, is you. You used to be proud of your standards. Now you're defending Mitch — the places he takes you, the language he uses, and the attitude he has toward us and everything we stand for. It can't go on like this."

Caryl patted her mother on the shoulder. "Don't make such a big deal out of it, Mom. I'm a big girl now. I can take care of myself." She changed the subject to her job, the money she was making, and the minor repairs the Ford needed.

That night Maryann told Bill, "I'm afraid Mitch is winning the war. We may be losing our daughter. When Martin and Brenda left home and got married, it was sad, but we rejoiced with them, too. But if Caryl leaves like this, it would be only tragedy." Even after praying together that God would protect Caryl both from herself and from Mitch, neither of them slept well.

The rest of the summer, Caryl was increasingly preoccupied — "she looks like she's in a dream world," said Maryann. Bill noticed that her comments about people in the church were all negative — "They're a bunch of losers," "I'm glad I'm not going to church every Sunday anymore," and "The people in the bars are friendlier than the people in your church." That shook Bill.

When the young couples Sunday school class invited him to speak at their annual "family life" retreat, he declined, even though he had enjoyed doing so in the past. "It would be pure hypocrisy for me to talk on family life, especially on parenting, when we are failing with one of our own children." Even his enthusiasm for preaching was gone.

By the middle of August, when Caryl started talking about trying to find a job in Dry Lake after graduation, Bill and Maryann decided something had to be done — even something drastic.

"We may be writing off our daughter," said Bill. "But unless something is done, we've lost her anyway. We've got to do something, even if Caryl leaves us, to restore the emotional stability of this home."

He sat down to think of all the leverage points he had with his daughter, who was now less than a year away from college graduation and complete independence. He put his thoughts into a letter.

Dear Caryl,

Sometimes being a parent is close to pure joy — like watching you take your first steps, taking part in your baptism, celebrating your selection as yearbook editor, or seeing you living out your faith as a college freshman.

Other times being a parent means having to make some difficult decisions, and now is one of those times.

Caryl, your mother and I feel like we're losing you. You think you are old enough to make your own decisions, but we'd like to think the way you were raised would have some influence on those choices. Over the past two years, we've talked repeatedly about your relationship with Mitch. Your family backgrounds, religious backgrounds, and personalities are incompatible. We cannot accept him in our family. And you would soon be torn between living in two worlds.

We've asked you to break it off. You have refused. You have said, "I'm old enough to make my own decisions." Maybe so. But if you continue in this relationship, Caryl, we will assume this means you are ready to make those decisions — and accept their consequences. You will always be our daughter, but once you remove yourself from under our guidance, there will be certain changes in our relationship.

1. You will no longer have use of the family car. We will expect you to return the Fairmont immediately.

2. I will tell the church board we no longer need the $1,000 scholarship the church provides you each year.

3. My own financial support of your education will end.

4. During your upcoming internship this year, you will not live in our house, as previously assumed, but you will find and furnish your own apartment.

5. Upon graduation, you will not be living with us "until a job opens up" but immediately be on your own.

As you learned to say in your self-assertiveness courses, Caryl, "I'm a self-made woman." Perhaps you are. I just thought you should know all that's involved if you persist in being your own person.

Let us know by August 30 if you prefer life with Mitch or life as part of our family.

Sincerely,

Dad

The Harrises mailed the letter, and three days later, August 27, Caryl called. "Well, I got your letter yesterday," she said.

"Have you done anything about it yet?" Bill asked.

"I thought I had some time."

"You have three days. We have to settle this, Caryl."

"I know, Dad." Caryl was subdued as she hung up.

Maryann noticed the strain on her husband's face. "She still wants to play both sides," she said.

"Yes, and I'm removing the option of the second side," he said.

In less than ten minutes, the phone rang again. It was Caryl. She was crying.

"I just called Mitch and told him it's over. I told him I'd gotten a letter from my dad and that I knew I had to decide between him and my family. And I realize I love my family more. So I did it . . ." She broke off in sobs.

"Do you want us to come be with you tonight?" Maryann asked.

"Yes."

Immediately Bill and Maryann packed a few things and drove the two hours to be with Caryl. When they arrived, Caryl hugged them both, but weakly. *She looks wrung out,* thought Bill. *But then, I feel like a wet noodle, too.* Over dinner, Caryl asked, "If I've done the right thing, why does it feel so bad?"

Bill and Maryann tried to affirm her decision. "You must feel torn apart," Maryann said. "You've chosen one side of who you are — the way you've been raised. It's painful when another side of you is cut out."

"We don't mean to be cruel or to punish you," said Bill. "We're simply trying to clarify what has really been taking place. Caryl, I'd rather hurt you now than to see you torn apart in a miserable marriage five years down the road."

After that emotionally draining crisis, the Harrises hoped everything was over, but their resolve continued to be tested. One Sunday afternoon when Caryl was home and Bill was away speaking at another church, Mitch called, inviting Caryl to meet him at a friend's apartment across town.

"Can't I go?" she asked her mom.

Maryann's throat felt dry. She wondered how Caryl could ask after all they'd been through. "I thought we agreed everything was over."

"But I need to talk to him. If I can't go there, can he come here?"

"I wish you wouldn't, but you do what you think is right."

Caryl told Mitch to come on over. Within fifteen minutes, Mitch was saying, "We're going out to a movie."

"I can't allow that," said Maryann.

"Don't you think Caryl's damn well old enough to make up her own mind?"

"When it comes to certain things, no," said Maryann, surprised at her own bluntness. "We've made it clear we don't think this relationship will work, and we don't see any point in you taking her out. If you need to talk, you can do it right here."

Mitch and Caryl went into the family room and sat on the couch. Maryann walked by and noticed Mitch's arm around

Caryl. They looked quite cozy. Taking a deep breath, she walked in and said, "Mitch, I don't know if you realize the importance of what Christ has done in our lives and what it means to us to be Christians, but I'd like to explain it if you're interested."

"Go ahead."

Maryann had just finished her church's evangelism training course and went through the whole presentation of the gospel. When she finished, Mitch said, "That's what I believe too. But, dammit, I get tired of having it crammed down my throat!"

"I'm sorry if it sounds like preaching," said Maryann. "But we try to live according to the Bible, and it commands us not to be 'unequally yoked' to those who don't share our commitment to Christ."

"My family worships God," said Mitch. "I don't see why you worship an old book written back in the 1300s."

Maryann chose to overlook the historical error.

"We feel there's another way to live when Christ becomes the Lord of your life. You live either to please him or to please yourself. That's why we think you and Caryl would have serious problems down the road."

"Hell, Caryl's no different from me."

"That remains to be seen. At least the way she's been raised is different from your lifestyle. You've made fun of her friends; you've made fun of her church and her parents; you've tried to undermine our relationship with her. It seems to me you're pulling her down instead of building her up. You once said you were attracted to Caryl because of her strong morals, because she was different from other girls you dated. It looks to me like you're trying to change her from the very thing that attracted you in the first place."

He looked a little surprised but said, "My parents weren't for this relationship at first, either. But they met Caryl and learned to like her. I don't see why you can't do the same."

"Mitch, you've taken her places she wouldn't have gone otherwise. She never dated anybody who drank or who used the language you use. Just sitting here tonight, five times you have used language we find vulgar or blasphemous," and Maryann repeated the words. Mitch's mouth dropped open. "You seem to be content with that. That's your lifestyle, but it isn't ours, and I don't think Caryl would be content with it either."

"You have no right to judge me. You're the most closed-minded people I've ever met."

"I don't mean to judge. I just wanted you to hear our side."

The conversation turned to other, less volatile topics, and Mitch showed no sign of leaving. Maryann didn't budge either. *If they stay until three in the morning, I'm staying here too,* she thought. But finally, after midnight, she said, "Well, I think it's about time you left, Mitch, because Caryl has to get up early to head back to school, and she really needs her rest."

I can't believe I'm doing this, she thought. *I've never asked anybody to leave my home before. But if he's exerting emotional energy, I will too.*

Mitch was civil as he got up and said good-bye. Afterwards Caryl, who had been silent throughout the evening, said, "I was terrified, Mom. Whenever I tried to talk with him like that, he'd tell me to shut up. I hope he listened."

"Me too, dear," said Maryann. "Me, too."

But even that was not the final encounter. Bill's resolve was also tried when two weeks later, he drove home from the church one afternoon to find a pickup truck in the driveway and Mitch talking with Caryl on the front steps.

"I had only the distance from the intersection to the house to find some emotional equilibrium," Bill said later. "I was fearful. I was angry. I was disappointed because we couldn't seem to get this thing behind us. Mitch insisted on coming by, and Caryl didn't have the strength to say no. So I had to play the bad guy."

Bill pulled into the driveway. As he walked to the front door, he tried to keep his voice from shaking. "Mitch, what are you doing here?"

"Just a social visit," said Mitch.

"I'm going to have to ask you to leave."

"Why? Let's go inside and talk about it."

"There's nothing left to talk about, Mitch. I resent your appearing here when we've given you a full explanation before."

"What about Caryl? Doesn't she have a say?"

"I'll talk to her when you're gone," said Bill.

"Shouldn't I be a part of it?"

"No, Mitch. That's just it; you're not a part of it." Bill paused, because as a pastor the next words were some of the most difficult he'd ever had to say. "You are no longer welcome in this house. I don't want to see you here again."

"Well I've stayed away for three weeks."

"Mitch, you don't cut off a dog's tail a little bit at a time. It's time you left."

"Damn you!" Mitch shouted, his face fiery red. Unused to facing a will as strong as his, he stormed out to his pickup, and his departure left rubber on the driveway.

Inside the house, Bill found Maryann crying, Caryl pale, and his voice quivering. "Caryl, why was he here?"

"He phoned to ask if he could come over, and I said yes."

Bill shook his head. "Why do you think I wrote that letter a month ago? Caryl, maybe it's time you moved out. I'd thought we'd reached the bottom line, but apparently we haven't."

Caryl's eyes filled with tears.

"I don't know what you want with your life or which way you want to go. But we are at the end of our emotional tether. We can't go any further. And if it means you're not going to be a part of our family any more, we're prepared to face that, even though we don't want to. But we cannot have this emotional warfare continuing. We're that serious. I don't want to see him in this house again."

"I can't make any decision right," Caryl sobbed. "Anything I do is wrong. You're disappointed in me. Why should I go on living? I'm good for nothing."

"Caryl, Caryl," Maryann said softly, holding her daughter's hand. "That's not true. It's because we think so much of you that we've done this."

"You've got too much to offer to throw away on a guy like Mitch," said Bill. "The only reason you've lost confidence in yourself is because for three years Mitch has been tearing you down. He's made your decisions for you. He's a mood-altering drug, and when he gets out of your system, you'll be able to make good decisions again."

For the next year, Bill and Maryann had to repeatedly prop up Caryl's sagging self-worth. But they persevered, and Mitch at last stopped his attempts to see Caryl. Gradually Caryl returned to the confident, independent thinker she had been.

Now, four years later, she has thanked her parents several times for stopping her from making a big mistake. She's the manager of a fabric store and helping direct the high school ministry in her local church.

"We took drastic action," Bill said. "It wouldn't have been successful if there weren't a hundred messages, a thousand messages, before that we loved her and truly wanted the best for her. We risked our twenty-year investment in family building. We clipped our emotional coupons with Caryl, and this is something you can do only once. It's not a threat you can use over and over. I'm not sure it would be the right approach for everyone, but in our case, it was the right move."

When You Risk the Relationship

Bill and Maryann Harris faced a unique situation with a daughter who did not want help with a particular relationship. Not everyone will encounter the same factors. Not everyone will choose to handle even similar situations the same way the Harrises did. But the story of the Harris family does illustrate several transferable principles, some of which have been suggested earlier in this book, for helping those who don't want help. What were the things Bill and Maryann clearly did right?

1. *They showed support and love.* For almost twenty years, Bill and Maryann had built a strong relationship — with one another and with Caryl. Even when the tension came, they continued to support Caryl (though not her decisions) and maintained their relationship with her through months and years of nerve-wrenching conflict. They demonstrated their care for her even when they were knocking heads.

2. *They communicated clearly and specifically.* They told Caryl their reasons for disapproving of her relationship with Mitch, and they made clear their expectations for her to break it off. They did not simply hint at their feelings or speak in veiled, offhand comments. Clear communication is critical so that when the bomb is dropped, the person doesn't feel it's a complete surprise and knows how to move to keep from getting hit.

3. *They did not rush to judgment.* Bill and Maryann were slow to escalate the conflict, to raise the stakes. They reserved playing their trump — risking their relationship — until they had exhausted every quieter, more diplomatic means available. They refused to rely on drastic measures (or threats of them) until they were absolutely sure Caryl was on a destructive path and all other methods of helping her had failed. They went the second mile, and the third, and the fourth . . . before acting. Only then, when the risk of losing her through confrontation was less than the risk of doing nothing and letting her be hurt even more, did they put their relationship on the line.

4. *They showed the extreme measures were for her best interests.* As Bill put it, "I'd rather hurt you now than see you torn apart in a bad marriage five years from now." Bill and Maryann had carefully checked themselves to make sure their actions were motivated not out of self-protection but genuine concern for their daughter's welfare. Then they were free to tell her so with boldness and integrity.

5. *They gave her a choice.* Even when they wrote the admittedly drastic letter, Bill and Maryann respected Caryl's freedom and let her make the final decision. They could have written, "Because of your previous actions, we are now cutting you off financially. . . ." But they didn't. They spelled out the consequences of her actions and gave her the freedom to make her own decision accordingly.

6. *They set a time limit.* They gave clear boundaries to their position — the behavior desired, the course they would follow if it were not chosen, and the time limit for the decision. They didn't let the Sword of Damocles hang over Caryl's head forever.

7. *They backed the demands with resolve.* Bill and Maryann were prepared to take the necessary measures, as wrenching as they would be, if Caryl's choice went against them. Empty threats are worse than doing nothing at all. Both Bill and Maryann demonstrated their strength of will and their determination to follow through on their decision.

8. *They did not withdraw once the decision was made.* The Harrises did not begrudge Caryl the pain she had caused them. Once she had made her choice, they dropped everything and drove to see her. They supported her, helped her stand firm in her choice, and continued to intervene with Mitch. Choices are not made in an emotional vacuum. They require maintenance. Bill and Maryann offered themselves to help Caryl maintain her decision.

Helping people who don't want help usually does not get to the point where the relationship must be risked, fortunately, but when the situation arises, these principles point the way to the greatest chance of success.

EPILOGUE

*One does not surrender a life in an
instant. That which is lifelong can only
be surrendered in a lifetime.*

JIM ELLIOT

Taking the initiative, stepping into ministry situations
uninvited, is rarely comfortable. But as the examples in this
book show, God does often honor the efforts of those who
genuinely try to help redeem a sad situation.

At times, however, we have to admit that when a person
consistently and persistently refuses our attempts to help,
there is a limit to what we can do. Manipulation and coercion
may change behavior, but it is beyond our power to directly
change others' attitudes and responses — the foundation
blocks of maturity.

Even Jesus Christ did not get through to everyone. "He
came to his own, and his own received him not," reports his
disciple John. When the people from the region of the Gera-
senes asked Jesus to leave (Luke 8:37), he got in a boat and left.
Despite his perfect love, wisdom, and patience, Jesus refused
to violate a person's freedom to choose. The capacity for self-
direction is one of God's great gifts to human beings — yet it's
a gift that can destroy us.

In fact, the biblical doctrine of hell can be described as a person's choice to be excluded from the presence of God. Often that hell begins in this lifetime.

"I think of the promiscuous young women I know," writes A. N. Wilson, "their faces already raddled with late nights, messy love affairs, and too much dope and drink, and compare them with the radiant calm of some of the Christian women I know. In such reveries, the Sermon on the Mount, with all its apparent reversal of common sense, seems luminously sane. . . . Why is it, the older one grows, the more topsy-turvy the wisdom of Christ appears; and yet the more it appears to be wisdom? He seems to be looking at life upside down; he tells us that the poor have security, the mourners will be happy, the sexually deprived will be the most fulfilled. It seems, by the wisdom of this world, as if he got everything the wrong way around. But live a bit, and one discovers that this is not necessarily the case at all. If the world is inverted, then the only way to see it clearly is upside down."[1]

Our task is to try, with all the loving means at our disposal, to keep people from choosing a hell on earth or the hell to come. Even though God-given autonomy guarantees individuals the freedom to respond to us as they choose, we can exert tremendous influence by our actions and attitudes. This book has looked at various strategies for doing that. But at times, pastors find they can do no more. They've reached the limit of their effectiveness.

When that moment comes, it is time for two prayers.

One, to use Hannah Whitehall Smith's term, is "a prayer of relinquishment."

As one pastor says, "At times, all I can do is tell God that I've done all I can at this point. I'm still available, and I've let the person know the door is always open, but it appears that God is going to have to cause the breakthrough. I tell God that I'm trusting his timing. I'm willing for my failed attempt to be simply one link in the chain of events God is forging for this person. I recognize I may be the first link or the twenty-first link, but very rarely am I God's last link in the chain."

The prayer of relinquishment is not a prayer of resignation. Rather than giving up, it's transferring the direct responsibility to God, recognizing the vast repertoire he has for reaching people, and waiting for him to take the initiative. It means being willing to re-enter the situation when the opportune moment comes.

The second prayer is for "God's astringent grace" for the person who refuses to admit his need.

"I don't have any right to pray that God will clobber someone," says a long-time counselor. "But I pray that he might bring crisis and difficulty. Sometimes in pain, people realize their need. I pray that God, in his mercy, will order the circumstances and deal with them in whatever way will make their lives happily productive for his purposes."

When a person's human relationships are falling to pieces, often it's because the primary relationship — the person's relationship with God — has been neglected. One pastor observed how easily these days people separate the experience of joy from the God who wills that "my joy may be in you, and that your joy may be full" (John 15:11). Eugene Peterson writes, "Joy, separated from its roots in God . . . becomes mere sensation. It is as easy to separate experiences of joy from God as it is to separate experiences of suffering from God. If the result of the latter is bitterness, the result of the former is boredom. Our culture has appointed the entertainment and leisure industries as guides to the experience of joy. But they are blind guides."[2]

Only by reuniting the pursuit of joy with the source of joy will any lasting satisfaction be found. This, ultimately, is the essential message of anyone trying to help those who don't want help.

---

1. A. N. Wilson. *How Can We Know? An Essay on the Christian Religion.* (New York: Atheneum, 1985).
2. Eugene Peterson. *Five Smooth Stones for Pastoral Work.* (Atlanta: John Knox, 1980) p. 159.

BIBLIOGRAPHY

Aycock, Don M. *Apathy in the Pew: Ministering to the Uninvolved*. Johnson City, Tenn.: Institute of Social Sciences and Arts, Inc., 1983. Suggests strategies for reaching those who don't care about receiving help. Focuses not on coercion but on "bathing persons in the good news of Christ."

Backus, William. *Telling Each Other the Truth*. Minneapolis: Bethany House, 1985. The author, a pastor and counselor, demonstrates how to improve relationships by telling the truth in loving ways.

Cerling, Charles, Jr. *Freedom From Bad Habits*. San Bernardino, Calif.: Here's Life Publishers, 1984. Dissects the dynamics of habitual behavior, often one of the factors involved in those resisting help.

Dale, Robert D. and Delos Miles. *Evangelizing the Hard-to-Reach*. Nashville: Broadman, 1986. Describes and offers case studies of reaching four kinds of people: the Left-Outs, the Drop-Outs, the Locked-Outs, and the Opt-Outs.

Davis, Creath. *How to Win in a Crisis*. Grand Rapids, Mich.: Zondervan, 1976. Fresh insights and illustrations of helping individuals struggling with personal conflicts, alcohol, emotional disturbances, and moral failure.

Knutson, Gerhard. *Ministry to Inactives*. Minneapolis: Augsburg, 1979. Discusses the art of Christian caring for those out of touch with the caring community.

Larsen, Earnie. *Stage II Recovery: Life Beyond Addiction*. Minneapolis: Winston, 1985. How to help the chemically dependent move from mere abstinence to full recovery.

Lenters, William. *The Freedom We Crave*. Grand Rapids, Mich.: Eerdmans, 1985. Treats addiction not as a chemical problem but a people problem. Deals with the addictions to romantic relationships, alcohol, food, fitness, work, and even unhealthy religious experiences.

Monfalcone, Wesley R. *Coping with Abuse in the Family*. Philadelphia: Westminster, 1980. Suggests ways to minister to both subtle and severe abusers.

Peterson, Eugene H. *Five Smooth Stones for Pastoral Work*. Atlanta: John Knox, 1980. Insights on the pastoral task based on studies of the Song of Songs, Ruth, Lamentations, Ecclesiastes, and Esther.

Schaller, Lyle E. *Activating the Passive Church*. Nashville: Abingdon, 1981. Diagnoses the various causes of passivity and offers a variety of methods for responding.

Spickard, Anderson, and Barbara R. Thompson. *Dying for a Drink*. Waco, Tex.: Word, 1985. One of the best books from a Christian perspective on dealing with the alcoholic.

VanVonderen, Jeffrey. *Good News for the Chemically Dependent*. Nashville: Nelson, 1985. Helpful insights into the mind of the person struggling with chemical dependency and how to assist in recovery.

Vredevelt, Pam, and Joyce Whitman. *Walking a Thin Line*. Portland: Multnomah, 1985. A handbook for helping those with anorexia or bulemia.

White, John, and Ken Blue. *Healing the Wounded*. Downers Grove, Ill.: InterVarsity, 1985. A call for firm but compassionate confrontation with sin in the church.

Worthington, Everett L., Jr. *How to Help the Hurting*. Downers Grove, Ill.: InterVarsity, 1985. Tells how to help people caught in their own pain to get to the root of the problem and deal with it constructively.